Soul Mission

*Establishing Your Life's
Strategic Priorities*

THE INTENTIONAL LIFE TRILOGY

BOOK TWO

Soul Mission

Establishing Your Life's

Strategic Priorities

Ramesh Richard

MOODY PUBLISHERS

CHICAGO

Unless otherwise marked, all Scripture quotations are taken from the HOLY BIBLE, NEW INTERNATION-AL VERSION®. Copyright © 1973, 1978, 1984 by the International Bible Society. Used by permission of Zondervan Bible Publishing House. All rights reserved. The "NIV" and "New International Version" trade-marks are registered in the United States Patent and Trademark Office by International Bible Society. Use of either trademark requires the permission of the International Bible Society.

Scripture quotations marked (KJV) are taken from *The Holy Bible,* King James Version.

Produced with the assistance of The Livingstone Corporation (www.LivingstoneCorp.com). Project staff includes Neil Wilson, Ashley Taylor, Mary Horner Collins, Dan Van Loon, Rosalie Krusemark.

Library of Congress Cataloging-in-Publication Data

Richard, Ramesh. 1953–
    Soul mission: establishing your life's strategic priorities/Ramesh Richard.
    p. cm. — (The intentional life trilogy; bk.2)
Includes bibliographical references.
    ISBN 0-8024-6461-0
1. Christian life. 2. Self-actualization (Psychology)—Religious aspects—Christianity. I. Title.
    BV4501.3.R53 2004
    248.4—dc22
                                                                                    200302176

1 3 5 7 9   10 8 6 4 2

Printed in the United States of America

To

Ron Crosby

A peer-level hero

Your spirit is contagious,
Your words thoughtful,
And your perspective is eternal.

You personify the heart of this book
in personal, family, and business life.

Thanks for generously investing with me
in the Ultimate, Unshakeable Economy.

Contents

Note from Author

The Intentional Life series focuses on restructuring our lives from randomness to intentionality and is divided into three sections: *Passion, Mission,* and *Vision.* Each segment arrives with a prologue, continues explanation with illustration, and calls for a personal response.

Hopefully, you have already digested Book One, *Soul Passion.* If you haven't, I encourage you to read through it. This second book in the trilogy, *Soul Mission,* examines the structure of building an Intentional Life based on the foundation we laid in the first book. Without your intentional acceptance of that foundation, your understanding of the house we are building will be lacking its most fundamental level.

I invite you to read this book twice. The first time read it with a pen in hand. Use the narrow margins to scribble out your comments and reactions. Interact with me, understand the arguments, predict and critique me. Then read it again with a notebook open. Dialogue with God. Write out your thoughts. You may even find supernatural resources for an Intentional Life in that interaction. I look forward to hearing from you at www.rreach.org.

Anchoring Life

For nearly five years my family and I lived in New Delhi, India. Dotting the neighborhood were several general store merchants. Naming their shops after family, such as "Patel & Sons," they announced their lineage, heritage, and experience. However, the subtitle of "General Store" on the shop sign described their business. General purpose merchants sold everything necessary for daily living: wheat, rice, toothpaste, razor blades, lightbulbs, candy, and aspirin. If you shopped there, you could meet each day's needs. Store owners maintained an inventory of ingredients required for basic survival. We shopped at these places nearly every day.

> Look well to this day
> For it is life, the very best of life
> In its brief course lie all realities and
> truths of existence
>   the splendour of warmth
>   the glory of power
> For yesterday is but a memory
> Tomorrow is only a vision
> But today, if well lived, makes
> every yesterday a memory of happiness
> and every tomorrow a vision of hope
> Look well therefore to this day.
>
> ❧ANCIENT SANSKRIT POEM

Specialty shops flourished nearby, supplying the market-place with items outside the scope of the general stores. Butchers, barbers, and bakers carried distinctive products or performed occasional services. These more exotic businesses catered to those who had a little extra to spend toward a special need (haircut) or a special day (a birthday cake). For routine needs we visited a general store. For special needs we shopped at the specialty stores.

A new economic day has dawned in Delhi since our time there. General purpose stores have expanded to carry specific merchandise. Indeed, some such stores have become known for what they carry in their upper floor departments. Distinctive items can be bought upstairs, but general-purpose merchandise still dominates the center of the "general" floor. You may ascend flights of stairs to buy specific, more expensive goods like Kashmiri carpets, but the ground floor features the staples for daily existence. The by-lines on the signs outside now proclaim that these stores are general and specialty merchants.

WHY DO WE NEED A PURPOSE?

The ground floor (or the first floor) of the store helps the business survive.[1] Money and people pour into that ground floor of the store on a regular, predictable basis. Unless there is a general purpose draw, the public won't come in. But the *specific purpose* merchandise coaxes them to climb the staircase to buy the high margin commodities. The business thrives from the upper-floor income.

Your life, too, needs to be constructed like those shop buildings, with general and special purpose levels. Built with God's universal and unique purpose in mind, such a life-structure will enable your effective existence and influence, helping you to survive and thrive, allowing you to be alive and finally arrive at its God-intended destination.

You need a general purpose, which

wakes you up each day,

nourishes your routines,

furnishes your sustenance,

provides you with motivation,

overcomes your monotony.

If you don't have one, you will be driven "out of business," so to speak. Without general purpose, the will shrivels. Without the will, will-ers wilt. Without the will-er—moral determination—there is no human purpose for life.

New Delhi's Municipal Authority is quite flexible if you want to continue adding on to a building straight up. Building codes are easily circumvented through bribes and corrupt maneuvers. Indian businessmen find it easier to receive forgiveness than permission from government bureaucracy (just like my children try to find with me). If a business owner wants to expand his or her operations, there is virtually no limit to the height of the building. But physics can't be bribed. At a certain point, the foundation must be reinforced in order to support the weight of a taller structure. The subtitles on the marquee have to be lengthened and the name boards widened to acknowledge the new expanded services available within. But if the store owner has a vision to pursue, there is no limit to how high he or she can go, *as long as the foundation can support and the ground floor can anchor that vision.*

In like fashion, a foundational passion governs you, a total mission grounds you, and a personal vision grows you into the heights as you move along into the future. That, in a sentence, summarizes what it means to live the Intentional Life.

DEFINING SOUL MISSION

May I help you articulate a general purpose for your daily existence so you can "look well to this day"? Will you explore with me what the general purpose—the ground floor—is for your life? A general purpose, like your life passion, will be sweeping, comprehensive, and extensive. It gives you the primary drive and pull for your daily survival and life's challenges. It fits as a constituent of the highest purpose.

At your death, eulogists may recall your mission in their panoramic descriptions of your existence. Your family may tearfully and proudly admit your life mission to the public—and be truthful about it. They may even inscribe your general purpose on your tombstone over your final passive, resting place on earth. But none of these results will probably occur unless you give serious thought and willful action to your general purpose for living—your *soul's mission*.

Soul mission is the outworking of humanity's essential reason for existence. Later in Book Three we'll explore how to build your "specialty" level—your unique features and specific vision in life. But now we will focus on a general purpose for life. Your current life mission relates to

what you do repeatedly,

what justifies your existence,

what validates your activity.

Whatever aspects of your life that fit the above conditions define your "mission." You may have inherited or unintentionally developed it, but your mission it is!

Your honest appraisal may produce some embarrassment. I am amazed how often I discover that very busy people stay very busy, in part, because they fear facing the truth about the worthlessness of their frantic busyness. Until you take the time to consider the repeated actions or habits in your life and the ways you have justified your existence and validated your activities, you won't have a clear sense of what must change. Experience intentional living to reflecting on this book and considering your present mission. Ask God to clarify and, if necessary, to redirect your purpose for life.

A wealthy man once contracted with a builder to construct the best house money could buy. His instructions were simple: spare no expense. But the builder decided he could make a handsome extra profit from this lavish contract. He used inferior materials. He hired inexperienced workers and approved shoddy workmanship. He cut corners everywhere that couldn't be seen. The result was a house that looked magnificent on the outside but was poorly built and dangerous to live in. The builder knew that.

The rich owner arrived for the final inspection of his new dream home. Walking through the house, he announced to the builder, "When I asked you to build this house, I actually wanted to give you a special gift. I knew how much you needed a house. Here are the keys. The house is yours."

God has given you the opportunity to build a house—a life—that is uniquely yours. You want to build it well. A spiritual foundation of *passion*—the love of Christ—equips you for balance, direction, and impact during life's brief building process. Your *mission*—general purpose—derives from your overall passion and becomes the ground floor of your daily life. Your unique *vision* will then summon your mission as you build a magnificent house on the inside as well as the outside.

Let's pursue the worthwhile task of profiling a Christian's

soul mission, or your general purpose, the first floor of life's building. It deals with your mission today, for this very day, and every day.

Extending Passion, Framing Mission

Early morning air travel is especialy difficult after truncated nights. But she sat next to me on a 7:00 a.m. Dallas–New York flight, eager to make conversation. She asked where I was going. As a rule, I go wherever the plane goes, so I replied, "New York."

She congratulated me for getting a good seat with extra leg space. She knew the dimensions of our seats, including the seat pitch and knee room. She quickly demonstrated familiarity with the seating configurations on every plane her favorite airline operated. She had called to arrange meal preferences and knew the number of drinks and food service this flight would feature. I thought she was a stewardess incognito.

> "I'll huff, and I'll puff, and I'll blow your house down."
>
> THE WOLF, FROM THE THREE LITTLE PIGS

I asked where *she* was going.

"Nowhere in particular!"

"Aren't you going to New York?"

"No. Actually, I traveled on the red-eye from San Diego last night to Dallas. This morning I am headed on to New

York. Later this afternoon, I go to Cincinnati, spend the night there. Then I'll catch an early flight to Salt Lake City and end up in San Diego tomorrow evening."

I repeated her travel route. She was amazed by my short-term memory, and I was amazed at her routing. "Why didn't you just stay home?"

"Well, I needed these flights and miles to keep up my status with the airline," she explained.

I expressed her statement in the form of a question. "You are spending all this time, energy, and money to keep up your mileage status with the airline?"

"You're right! You really do have an amazing recall."

Perplexed, I said again, "You are spending all this time, energy, and money to keep up your mileage status with the airline." And then I added. "What a powerful parable for life! Spending precious resources to keep up perceived status. May I use your story?"

"Sure, sure," she said, though I'm sure she thought I was going to use her as a positive motivation for living.

Many people expend energy, time, and money to keep up their status—spending resources they don't have in order to get status that they don't need so they can impress people they don't know. My seatmate's "mission" in life at that point was to keep her status with the airline, and she spent her resources accordingly.

A central question that your soul mission asks and answers is: "Why do you do what you repeatedly do?" It will take some time to identify those actions and habits. What do you do almost every day? How do you approach most people or situations? Listing these "constants" as your mission in life will help you see them in a new way. Redirect your thinking if you have already forced yourself into a forged but unexamined mission for life. You may have been trapped by counterfeit values, beliefs, and conduct. You may be trying to live someone else's life mission. Or you may be living in the chaos of inherited and collected mission fragments from many others. Since the genuine mission of your life will arise from the passion of your life, we need to frame or reframe your mission, making sure that it fits the foundation of the passion we have already explored.

In *Soul Passion* (Book One of this series) we broke ground for an extended illustration of the Intentional Life. Here let me summarize and expand the earlier proposition. Borrowing from Jesus' parable of the wise and foolish builders (Matt. 7:24–27), we connected the construction of a physical dwelling to building a life. Indeed, the principles of interior, physical design in buildings also correspond to an interior spiritual redesigning of life. Interior design significantly influences the exterior life. Many live an exterior life without an adequate interior spiritual pattern, yet others live without any conscious, internal pattern at all. In either case, they live on different assumptions than the intentional, patterned life. They are examples of what we called living randomly.

We began with life's foundation—your absolute passion forms your ultimate purpose. But your ultimate purpose demonstrates its presence and vitality throughout the rest of the structure you are constructing. Soul passion provides pervasive, foundational strength for life. In review, Book One stated that every part of the structure of life in some way acknowledges its connection to the foundation. In preview of the rest of this present book, we will see how the mission (your general purpose) of an intentional life is framed and structured by that foundation of passion. Let's extend the metaphor and truth of passion into a framework for life mission.

Floors, walls, and ceilings are found on every level of every house. In order to communicate the comprehensive, connected, and critical role of passion, I now choose the floor/wall/ceiling metaphor to describe both the identity and function of personal passion on setting up for life's mission. Each of these brings benefits and places boundaries to life. As I intimated before, passion influences our assumptions, focuses our choices, and guides our behavior. It will define and frame our sole mission, our soul's mission.

FLOORS

Floors are part of the basic structure of a house. I am not speaking of floor coverings—uniquely chosen, laid, relished, and used according to personal taste. Floor coverings are laid onto the floor structure. Floor structure is always there—beneath the tile, wood, and the carpet. It seems passive. It is indispensably necessary. It relentlessly supports. A beautiful carpet laid over a gaping hole or damaged floor joists may look pleasing—until we step on it. We depend on floor structure. There is no way around it!

Now that I think about it, the floor is the most under-appreciated, neglected part of my house. I don't have to hold it up. I don't make it function. I only take notice of the floor when I spill something, when it gets dirty, or when tiles separate. For the most part it is simply there, unnoticed. But I couldn't get far in my house without it.

Passion functions in the manner of floor structures. The floor framework extends the strength of passion (the foundation) by creating a supporting span upon which we walk and work. Our passion includes our worldview—the assumptions we hold about life and reality. Passion supports and shapes our worldview at every level, every decision, and every activity. In the psychology and sociology of religion, we speak about worldview as the control box of individual and cultural behavior. Seeing the connection between passion and worldview, then, becomes crucial to the Intentional Life. Like floors, passion influences and controls our way of life without becoming that life. It can't replace life; it receives what we place on it. On occasion we need to clean it up, for passion dirties with spills. If the spiritual foundation shifts, the fractures appear in floor-passion.

We use floors. We don't make them useful. We assume them. Unlike basements, we don't have to make floors functional.[1] We may cover them with carpet or layer them with linoleum, but these are surface changes. The most beautiful floor coverings—Alpujarra rugs from Spain, Chinese Ningsia tapestries, or marble granite quarried in India's state of Rajasthan—simply decorate the surface of a floor. We live off floor dimensions. Similarly, passion doesn't live by us; we live off our passion. Like floors, passion functions all the time.

The way we experience passion compares to the floor structure in a dwelling. Our passion may be enhanced with appropriate coverings, but we can't extend its quality or expand its competency. Quality and competency come from the divine Savior-architect while it is being built.

Likewise, the quality and competency of a worldview derives from its attachment to truth. When we speak about a biblical worldview, we are attempting to explain and justify our assumptions over and against other assumptions. The deity, exclusivity, necessity, sufficiency, and authority of the Lord Jesus Christ found and are founded on those basic assumptions. For instance, the Christian worldview demands a theistic sense (where humans are not God). Monistic assumptions (where all reality is one essence), pantheistic assumptions (where humans exhibit divinity), or deistic assumptions (where divinity absconds from human life), all conflict with the uniqueness of Jesus as God. Consequently, our inferences about reality contradict inferences from nonbiblical assumptions. Christians hold that it is possible for God and humans to share in life without abandoning their distinctiveness. Passion, informed by justifiable assumptions, elicits the total, spiritual, love response of the believer to Jesus, without either losing their identities or functions. In a fundamental way, the passion of the Christian centers on the Lord Jesus Christ.

In *Soul Passion* we looked at Jesus Christ's work of salvation as the foundation on which we build life, and His values as the foundation by which we live. In this book, we reference the person of Jesus as our ground floor as well, the underlying structure of our lives. He is not only the Giver of life but also the ground-floor anchor of life's growing building. He remains our constant support wherever we move in life. He functions as the solid ground on which we carry out our soul's mission.

WALLS

Walls keep people and property safe. Walls also enclose space. Like floor coverings, wall surfaces can be paneled, painted, papered, or left in natural texture.

We find "room" within the walls, for walls create and define the rooms and other internal spaces. Think of passion that way. In addition to providing floorlike support, passion also provides space. It is liberating before it is constrictive. Passion gives us room to function, fill, and fulfill, or we wouldn't pursue multiple passions. Passion helps us dream, grow, and rearrange the furniture of life, or we wouldn't follow erroneous passions. Passion(s) function alike, regardless of the object of the passion. The worthiness of the object needs to be argued independently. Passion(s) operate in like manner. We only evaluate their validity—which object of passion is right, true, and beautiful?

Passion also matches the load-bearing task of walls. In addition to energizing our salvation foundation, vibrant spiritual passion also supports ongoing life. Passion keeps its occupants safer and supplies strength for life's endeavors. While room capacity differs from person to person, the burden of one's life is distributed over load-carrying passion as foundation-stabilizing spiritual disciplines intermingle.

Passion, like walls, creates a frame within which we must live. Like walls, passion also constricts. It forces you to make some choices. It views some things as invalid. It calls some choices wrong. It renders some issues irrelevant and makes other issues obsolete. Note the wisdom of Paul's passionate confession in early English, "For the love of Christ constraineth us" (2 Cor. 5:14 KJV). However, within the constraining framework of passion lies the fertility of an intentional Life. You may want to evaluate your present passion according to its virility, productivity, and fertility. Which passion provides true freedom for your life? Which passion provides an appropriate framework for your choices, activities, and future?

You will find the Lord Jesus to be the true foundation and the justifiable assumption for your life's floor structure. In Him you will find room to freely unleash your life as well as finding the framework to direct your freedom. He not only gives eternal life but also grounds our present life, generating a high-impact life. A passionate love for Jesus Christ overflows into an abundant, fruitful, useful life.

CEILINGS

Ceilings are the largest unbroken surface of most buildings. Ceiling decorations often are an afterthought in the interior design process. We usually embellish ceilings to cover their concrete structure and hide the ugly snarl of wiring and ducts. But ornate ceilings distinguish exquisite buildings. The world's most famous ceiling, in the Sistine chapel, adorns a rather plain building. Inside we are stunned by the most magnificent frescoes of master artists. Melbourne's National Gallery of Victoria boasts a historical and international collection of art, but nothing compares with the sensational stained-glass ceiling in its Great Hall.

Ceilings provide a wide surface to display designed effects. Thoughtful decorators alter simple ceilings to enhance lighting, to influence ambience, and even to affect feelings. Since low ceilings can cause claustrophobic depression, they are lit well. I walked into my study carrel at our school library one morning to find the lights out in my entire section. The low, plain, flat ceiling increased the sense of dreariness. After working that morning, I alerted the front desk about the problem for it was affecting my mood during an already intense period of writing. Now you know why this section is wearying to read! That electrical glitch made me appreciate the skill of a deliberate designer who planned lighting to help me work.

Could this physical design metaphor extend to the passion of a person? Certainly. You arrive in this world in certain colors and grow to particular dimensions. Competency and capacity are mostly wired in. However, you have the opportunity to light up your life by properly utilizing, limiting, even "painting" your ceiling of passion for maximum effect. The Intentional Life evidences a capacity for putting light in the right places.

Unless you have an anchoring and awareness of an interior spiritual redesign, don't even think about the Intentional Life. Unless the interior of your life-house is cared for and nurtured, don't worry about intentional living. An intentional life includes interior design and exterior strategy. To emphasize one over the other dislodges equilibrium and throws us off balance. But if you really have to choose to emphasize one over the other, choose an interior spiritual redesign.

SELF-IDENTITY: FROM PASSION TO MISSION

There is no limit to the creative expressions we can make in the choices of floor coverings, wall sidings, and ceiling displays. To a large extent, the design and décor of wall, floor, and ceiling surfaces of building our lives is left to our preferences, tastes, and abilities. Not only do humans display different passions, they also exhibit different abilities about similar passions. These naturally lead to a wide variety of missions. But the Bible proposes one *object* of human passion—God is to be our ultimate love because He is what we ultimately need and want as our first love. Every mission in life must derive its validity from the degree to which it expresses this central passion.

Philosophically, the material constituents of passion can be the same. We all can choose to what we will give significance in our lives. God is the only justifiable choice we can make, and therefore He provides the structure for our identity and the identity of our life structure. Unlike my copassenger on the New York flight who derived some self-worth from airline mileage status, we root our *self-identity*—not self-esteem nor self-worth nor self-love, but self-identity—in the rock-hard concrete of who we are in Jesus Christ.

I can't emphasize the biblical nature of Christian identity

enough. Too many of us solicit our identity from the signifi
cance of our function (capacity and ability). Our function i
a part of identity but is by no means its root or entirety.[2]

When we start making the pursuit of "significance" a cor
component of our identity, we will be frustrated—we wil
never be significant enough. Or we will arbitrarily wait for a
latter part of life when we will really find significance. The
there is the problem of not knowing if we are guaranteed a
latter part of life! Also, the Bible never asks us to seek signifi
cance, nor is it promised. We are already significant to God
Instead of creating many ways to salvation, He loved u
enough to give us his Son for salvation, and His Holy Spiri
for spiritual power—all sources of spiritual self-identity no
based on utilitarian, pragmatic, or circumstantial significance

When we derive our identity from our passion founded i
Jesus' salvation, that significance in itself sustains u
throughout life, even in the face of ghastly personal, family
professional, or ministry failure. We give God and His worl
true significance in our lives and subscribe to an unshakabl
and true identity as a new creation in Christ Jesus. We le
Him be the ground and content of our significance.

While a passion for God—the first commandment of foun
dations, floors, walls, and ceilings—must form everyone's lif
structure, the abilities for passionate pursuits may diffe
according to the individual. These abilities identify us a
unique—just like everybody else! Passion covers our particula
identity and unique expression. How we fill the room spac
will show present function (mission) and future utility (vision)
We share the structure of passion with everyone else. We ca
choose right or wrong objects of passion and give them signif
icance in right or wrong ways. However, the internal design o
the house communicates our individuality. The material struc

ture of the home pulsates with the passion *of* our life. Passions *in* life expound the nature of our life. It is good to subsume the nature of our life under its right identity as a lover of God. Both mission and vision will reveal present function and future profitability to God and neighbor.

A CRITICAL DISTINCTION: IN OR OF?

Here I reintroduce a critical distinction we highlighted in Book One, *Soul Passion*. We can have many passions *in* life, but we must have only one passion *of* life. Since we are creatures of Scripture and culture, we must distinguish between the passion of life and passions in life. Jesus used the distinction (John 17:11) to describe our relationship to the world— to be in it, but not of it.[3] We don't belong to the world (John 15:18–19), but we are located in the world. By virtue of our historical and geographical location, we are afforded the privilege of soft passions—we live in the world. We do not deny the world; we are simply intentional about our in-the-world-ness. We enjoy many loves and love many enjoyments.

Reinhold Messner, mountaineering's "Mr. Extreme," describes himself in a magazine article as an "over-stepper of limits" because the greatest expanses of ice and the highest mountains are his world. Yet he is concerned about his passion in life being consumed by age, if not climbing legislations! He realizes he will have to replace mountain climbing with another passion, another "vision of tomorrow."[4] The biblical model permits and promotes changing passions *in* life, as long as they are not sinful, subsumed under an unchangeable passion *of* life. Together they reveal your passion *for* life.

You need to check on passions that are promoted and prohibited by Scripture. God has given us all things to enjoy (1 Tim. 6:17), but when we begin to love the things we ought to enjoy, we break a relationship. We are not to love the world nor the things that are in the world (1 John 2:15). But we may love people—spouses, neighbors, even enemies—*in* life promoted by Scripture. But any time a *thing* becomes a love, we worship idols. Anytime a legitimate love competes for first place with Jesus, we cease being faithful as disciples.

So we cannot pursue things as passions. We may enjoy every love, but not love every enjoyment. Further, we cannot enjoy approved passions as docile, compliant non-agents. We bestow and retract their role in our lives. A person can make a spouse (scripturally promoted) his passion *in* life, or he can make work (scripturally prohibited) his passion *in* life. When work claims passion status over family, it breaks with Scripture. When family and work compete, we must reorder life as a testimony to our ultimate passion for Jesus. We can decide in a biblical way how dominant or dormant any item in life is going to be. Again, only one person fits the category for passion *of* life, and the many passions *in* life must be organized and pursued under the direction of God—Jesus.

Notice also the change in number, from *passion* to passions. As our new spiritual environment of being in Christ (John 17:20–21) inevitably wins out over our old spiritual loyalties (the world system that opposes God), we process our previous passions through the filter of our consuming passion. The many passions in your life, usually dealing with interests and hobbies, probably at some time or other will cause you to object to God's being your singular, central passion. Does knowing God as your life's passion challenge and interfere with your life passions? He should. He immediately limits your involvement in immoral passions. He intrudes into morally permissible but idolatrous passions. But then knowing God as our soul passion also intensifies other passions that are legitimate.

To reiterate the thriving marriage dynamic we discussed in Book One—when your relationship with your beloved is robust, every other dimension of life seems to experience joy; when matters are not going very well between the two of you, every other aspect of life is clouded by that need. So don't be afraid of loving God passionately, for the passion after God turns into the resource for pursuing all your other right passions rightly. But if your passion for God isn't first priority, that deficiency limits your enjoyment of other passions. Reserve uppercase, bold **PASSION** only for God. The PASSION of life is not the same as passions in life. Pursue approved passions in life under the floored, walled, roofed passion for God. Passion for God provides borders with space, but can carry the load as high as you want to build.

GOD'S RESTORATION PROJECT

In terms of architecture, Prague easily ranks among the most beautiful cities in the world. For decades in the twentieth century the beauty of the city was veiled behind a Communist curtain. Wars, strikes, and other causes of deprivation enveloped the city's charm with undesirable residue. Czechs are understandably proud of their city. They were in for a huge surprise in the grand restoration project of the *Obecni Dum*. Even after it was trashed by German and Russian soldiers, it functioned as the community house in the German section of Prague for decades. When renovators went in, they found mounds of beer bottles on the floors. Walls were covered with soot and grease, and ceilings blackened by carbon. The state-financed restoration lasted from 1993 to 1997. Every tile on floor, wall, and ceiling was meticulously cleaned. The public anxiously awaited the outcome of the work.

When the building opened, long lines of people wound around the edifice—a wait of three or four days. The public was not disappointed. They entered the majestic atriums, the great halls, and the illustrious staircases and were stunned with the most extravagant murals on the walls—at every level. The fabulous art had been hidden behind the dust and dirt for many, many years. And, in the basement, a restaurant for tourists soon flourished as news of the revived wonder spread. When I visited, I was enthralled both by the building itself as well as by the obvious pride and delight of the citizens over their restored treasure.

If you have received the salvation of Jesus Christ, you, too, are being restored on the inside. But black carbon from competing passions continues to accumulate. Your inner beauty is hidden. Your ultimate purpose gradually disappears under the dust and trash of confusion and forgetfulness at every level of your life. You have replaced your passion for Jesus with idolatrous ones. The spiritual life process parallels a massive cleaning and restoration effort. When you confess your sins, Jesus is faithful and just to forgive *and* cleanse you (1 John 1:9). You are also being restored to intended, former glory—the recovery of the image of God in you, and the restoration of what He had begun in you by the power of the Spirit in your submission to His Word. The disciplines of the spiritual life not only preserve the foundation, they facilitate the restoration of your passion.

Every house boasts windows and doors. They open to let light shine in and let you look out. On pleasant nights in safe neighborhoods you swing them wide-open for fresh air. You don't want your life to be a completely encased cavern, without entries, exits, or lights. Even a maximum-security prison allows for a door. Imagine a home without windows or doors. Unless your insides are lit, you will get comfortable in the dark. Unless you let fresh air come in, you will get stuffy. All of us need windows and doors, even as we need floors, ceilings, and walls at every level. You can't live a vital life on a long-term basis in an enclosed type of situation. Let's go beyond the enclosed, encased life into the dimensions of life where we must live intentionally. Continue *Soul Mission* to build the *ground floor* of the Intentional Life.

Sole Mission

Every day Juan faithfully pushed his bike with a sandbag straddling the center bar across the Mexican-U.S. border. Repetition eventually aroused suspicion. U.S. border patrol stopped him, only to find sand. The agent knew Juan was smuggling something of value into the country, but couldn't quite figure out what it was. Spot-checking did not divulge contraband of any sort. In desperation one day, the frustrated agent made a deal with Juan: "I'll only ask you this question once. I'll never stop you again from entering the country. I know you are smuggling something in every day. What is it?"

> There is no part of our life or conduct, however insignificant, which should not be directed to the glory of God.
>
> ❧JOHN CALVIN

Juan answered, "Bicycles!"

The boy's singular mission was to smuggle bicycles. He used the sandbags to accomplish the mission. Like Juan, we too embark on a daily journey through the world, but too many of us make hauling sandbags the mission of our lives. We handle incidentals as if they were essentials. We confuse those who watch us, too. Unlike Juan, the same sandbag and bicycle we took with us in the morning returns with us at night, inseparable companions in an unintentional life. The sandbags of life's routine must not be confused with a worthy ulterior purpose in life. The intentional life finds, remembers, and daily accomplishes an ulterior mission.

SOLE PURPOSE

God's sole purpose for creation is lucid and loud throughout the Bible—to bring glory to Himself. All biblical truth points humanity to an ulterior purpose—to glorify God, to make God look great, to reflect His character, to spread His reputation, to please Him, to demonstrate His growing weight within human life.

Nonhuman creation, indeed, the entire cosmos, experiences little trouble ascribing glory to God. It can't help but deflect glory to its Creator. Yet humans sense conflict and obstacles in reflecting the glory of God, in returning glory to God. We are the only variable factor among creatures glorifying God. We tend to rob God of His glory by withholding the recognition and honor that He alone is worthy to receive. Yet in Scripture God's glory is the ulterior purpose of the human enterprise. God's glory has been the sole purpose of humankind from the very beginning. Whether that sole purpose will become *our* soul's purpose is the question and challenge.

Psalm 8 emphatically reveals God's ulterior purpose for *humanity*. This dynamic creation psalm features thrifty poetry and poignant statements. It echoes the preface (Gen. 1) of the Manufacturer's manual. It presents a grand and unified theory of intentional, human existence. It weaves human origin, identity, meaning, destiny, and morality together in a masterful marriage of thoughts and words, concepts, and precepts. The implications of this psalm are far-reaching for intentional human existence.

The one "thing," the sole mission, our ulterior purpose can be summarized thus: God made us so we can glorify God—so we can make Him look good through us. God made humans great in all creation so we can make God look great to all creation. Care to read that again? That proposition summarizes the central idea of Psalm 8. Later in the Bible we read that God makes humans good (chosen in salvation to be holy and blameless, Eph. 1:3–4), so believers can make God look great (for the praise of His glory, Eph. 1:6, 12, 14). But in Psalm 8, God's glory invested in us must convey His intrinsic glory to all reality. God creates and restores human beings to reflect His character and even echo His reputation on earth.

Two assertions about God's significant reputation in created reality are found in this charming psalm:

➤ The Creator's glory is reflected in nature (Ps. 8:1–2).

➤ The Creator's glory is expected of humans (Ps. 8:3–9).

Cosmic and creation purpose—the glory of God—must translate into human and personal life purpose.

GOD'S NAME REVEALS HIS GLORY

Psalm 8 begins with the assertion that God's glory is grasped on a cosmic scale.

O LORD, *our Lord,*

> *how majestic is your name in all the earth!*

You have set your glory

> *above the heavens.*

The name of God is majestic in all the earth. (Observe that this statement is repeated for emphasis and closure in verse 9.) The Hebrew people attached and anticipated character with names. We name children according to current trends only to find out that the name is no longer popular when, decades later, it seems to count! For instance, very few "Bonnies" (my wife's name) are found anymore, though I grew up singing (and believing), "My Bonnie lies over the ocean!" Or we name babies for rhyme, alliteration, and rhythm. Former Texas governor James Hogg named his daughter "Ima." An evangelistically eager Christian worker in Southern India named his son John Three Sixteen. Recent consultants have alerted expectant parents to watch for how initials may appear on a baggage tag or a monogram, as D.O.G or H.A.G would be embarrassing.

For the Hebrews, naming took on a covenant tone. To name someone carried powerful spiritual meaning. They didn't name people for convenience or cuteness, but for character. Even today we occasionally come across careful naming and self-naming acts. People take on new names to reidentify themselves. Some do it at religious conversion. Hassan Rameh changed his name to George Washington America since he was born at the George Washington University Hospital in Washington, D.C. He ran for the United States presidency in 1980 and 1992. Others demonstrate ethnic or cultural heritage in their naming and renaming processes.[1] During the Middle Ages, Jewish citizens in Poland and Russia were made to take German sounding names to set them apart. In Fiji, middle names often tell of an event that holds some importance either to the birth of the child or its parents. Have you noticed that *nicknames* are often more true to meaning and character?

In Psalm 8:1 the psalmist uses the double name for God, "LORD, our Lord," as a meaningful nickname. The repetition is for effect and meaning. This *One* is the *Super* Lord, *Only* Lord, Lord of Lords. One can't exaggerate or magnify his God too much. Our best attempts to embellish His greatness understate what truly is the case.

The divine double name is also spelled differently—LORD and Lord—setting the tone of the psalm. He is not only the covenant God of the nation, or locale, or for personal purposes. He is the Creator God for international, global, corporate purposes. How lofty and wide is His name in all the earth! A sovereign God who is interested and involved across the earth. His reputation is enhanced and enjoyed in all the earth. "The whole earth is full of His glory" (Isa. 6:3).

Naming was not only a cultural exercise filled with meaning, the naming of *God* in itself was unique to Israel's God. Israel lived in a world that held the divine to be an unnameable entity. Not unlike today's pluralistic world, those who proclaimed the unnameableness of God were seen to be philosophically astute and religiously sophisticated. Yet think with me about the concept of an unnameable God. An unnameable God yields a contradiction, for God's name would simply then be "the unnameable god." The city of Ouray in southwestern Colorado sits in the bottom of a valley amidst magnetic and majestic peaks. All the mountains except one around Ouray County have names. In publications and conversations, that unnamed mountain is named . . guess what? "Unnamed" (13,072 feet). In stark contrast to the times, both present and past, Israel's God had no problem naming Himself (cf. Ex. 3:14). Part of Israel's role as God's chosen covenant people involved knowing and promoting the name of God in a world of competing theologies. Character, ability, and personality were found in a Hebrew name. Israel's God was unique and exclusive in Himself, as well as necessary and sufficient to them. Their God was *Something Else! Some One Else!* Something else than human. *Some One* entirely other than other "gods."

CREATION REFLECTS GOD'S GLORY

The first verse of Psalm 8 goes on to exclaim that God's glory is set "above the heavens." From the earth the psalmist ascends the aerospace staircase to stratospheric heights. God has generously displayed His glory in the heavens.

I am an amateur dabbler in elementary astronomy. With so many radical and increasing revisions in the field of astronomy, I don't know how I will ever get out of the elementary stage! I must confess I am easily dazzled by the size and number of galaxies strewn across the heavens. The farther away they are, the faster these galaxies seem to fly. Astronomers don't know yet whether galaxies uniformly or lopsidedly recede from each other. They think they can measure the speed of this recession but don't know the distances from one galaxy to the other to make judgments with certainty.

One morning in January 1996, I woke up to find that scientists changed some critical numbers almost overnight. Changing the numbers shouldn't surprise us, but the magnitude and haste with which they changed basic numbers amazed those of us who were interested. For ten consecutive days in December 1995, while peeking through a keyhole into the known, inner sanctum of the universe, astronomers used the Hubble Space Telescope to take long exposure photographs deeper into space than ever before achieved. By concentrating on one especially narrow sector of the sky, they recorded a bewildering number and variety of galaxies stretching back toward the beginning of time. Stunned by the numerical data, they raised the universal count from 10 billion galaxies to 50 billion. Overnight! Couple that with the astonishing fact that the earth's sun is simply one of 50 billion to 100 billion stars in our Milky Way, generally considered to be an ordinary galaxy. They observed a slice of the heavens no wider than 1/25th of one degree, equivalent to the size of a grain of sand held at arm's length. Within that sliver of space they counted 1,500–2,000 galaxies. That was in 1996! Fact-oriented, hard-nosed scientists grew misty-eyed and excited as they watched radiation left over from the theorized origin of an explosive Big Bang event. Astronomy is no longer "twinkle, twinkle little star." Rather, it's twinkle in the wonderer's eye. In late 1998, astronomers raised the galactic number again to an awe inspiring 125 billion. And in early 2001 astronomers found "what may be the largest structure in the observable universe, an immense concentration of quasars and galaxies clustered across more than 600 million light years."[2] We definitely don't know this seemingly indefinite count of what we yearn to know.

Is this extravagant splendor part of the glory of God set "above the heavens"? That glory is more majestic than all we know. The more we come to know the grandeur of God, the more we will kneel in awe at His glory. Charles Spurgeon, the famous preacher, says of the English version of Psalm 8, verse 1: "No words can express that excellency; and therefore it is left as a note of exclamation."

Psalm 8 goes on to declare that God's glory is even known at a child's level (vs. 2).

From the lips of children and infants

> *you have ordained praise*

because of your enemies,

> *to silence the foe and the avenger.*

Even children are ordained to praise God's glory. Infants at their mother's breasts, who cannot independently sustain themselves (does anybody, anytime, anywhere, by any means, sustain themselves?) are ordained to ascribe glory to God. What adults do not do, children already do. Adults are *called* to ascribe glory to the Lord (cf. Ps. 29:1); children already bring glory to Him. They cannot bring sacrifices and offerings to Him as adults can. They don't sing to Yahweh as adults should. They can't submit to Him as adults will. However, they have already been ordained to praise Him as part of the created order.

Theologically, the concepts in this verse are potent. Individually and *en masse,* humans are not where we began, not fulfilling the purpose for which we were created or born. We cannot make sense of the universe without the Creator's interpretive grid of glory. God's glory revels in our infantile naiveté and openness. God uses our infancy to praise Himself. "You have ordained praise" can also be translated, "You have established strength." God's glory is not only seen in His cosmic establishment but also is spotlighted and strengthened at a child's level. The marvels of childishness and childhood unknowingly bring praise to God.

Meanwhile, we in independent adulthood (more hood than adult) ordain praise for ourselves. We've grown up, but wrongly. Adult pride may be why Jesus challenged His disciples to change and become like little children in order to enter the kingdom of heaven (Matt. 18:1–3). Unless we give up the conceit and self-love advanced in adulthood, unless we adorn the humility and other-love of trusting childhood, we will not enter the kingdom of heaven. For it is childlikeness, not childishness, that brings praise to God.

The psalmist remarks that children's praise has the effect of silencing the foe or confounding the enemy (see Ps. 8:2). The enemies of God put out an alternate refrain of glory: "O Self, O self, how majestic is my name in all the earth." God's opposers either passively or actively make a travesty of the majesty of God. Therefore, God appoints children's praise to inadvertently confound the sophistry of grown-ups. The apostle Paul rephrased this cosmic truth to the Corinthian Christians:

> But God chose the foolish things of the world to shame the wise; God chose the weak things of the world to shame the strong. He chose the lowly things of this world and the despised things—and the things that are not—to nullify the things that are, so that no one may boast before him (1 Cor. 1:27–29).

One example of a child confusing and confounding an adult is the story of the father who tried to inculcate atheism in his son. "Son, show me. Where is God?" asked the father, expecting no empirical proof of God's presence from his child.

The boy replied, "You first show me where God is not, Dad!"

Surprised, the father painted a "God Is Nowhere" poster and showed it to his son.

The boy haltingly read, "God is Now here," and then innocently queried, "Dad, does God know we are atheists?"

In that unguarded moment the atheist father replied, "Yes, He does."

In the New Testament Jesus quoted from the Greek version of Psalm 8. He had purified the temple. The blind saw. The lame walked. The leaders "saw the wonderful things he did and the children shouting in the temple" (Matt. 21:15) and they became indignant. Jesus reminded them of Psalm 8:2: "Have you never read, 'From the lips of children and infants you have ordained praise'?" (Matt. 21:16). Jesus not only claimed to be the LORD-Lord of earth-wide excellence, He referred to His opposition as the enemies of God.

The glory of God in creation then, extends from the cosmos to children. Will it emanate from your mouth? Will be exhibited through your life?

God's purpose for humans is to magnify the majesty of His name—not to enlarge it but to display how large His majesty actually is. Creation already does that. Children are appointed and utilized to do that. Will you do that? Will you honor Him, worship Him, glorify Him, reflect Him, rather than resisting His glory as your ulterior purpose in daily existence? His enemies resist that transfer of glory. They seek to rob His glory in and from any part of the earth. They reject His glory, having grown up into a measure of supposed independence. Will you stay childlike when it comes to glorifying God on a daily basis?

NAME THEOLOGY

I suggest you pick up a Bible concordance and trace the word "name" in reference to God throughout the Psalms. You'll notice that God's name and character are synonymous. You will discover a significant "name theology" replete with implications for the Intentional Life. Let me start you off with a couple of specific verses. You may jot some spiritual implications in the slender margins of this page.

To glory in His name (Ps. 105:3) is to

> *call on His name,* unlike unbelievers (Ps. 79:6; 80:18). What a privilege!

> *intercede for His people,* like Moses and Aaron (Ps. 99:6). What a responsibility!

> *make Him known,* among the nations (Ps. 105:1). What an opportunity!

There you are, with the privilege, responsibility, and opportunity to make God look great each day.

Look up a couple more "name" verses in the Psalms. The concordance at the back of your Bible will give you a good place to start. Write out one or more specific strategies for immediate obedience related to what you discover about the name of the Lord. If possible, do it now.

Here is another line of thought. God not only named Himself (Ex. 3:13–14) as the One who is (or will be), He also implicated Himself by proclaiming this unusual name in Exodus 34:6–7. Remember this is God's *self*-description, His "Who He Is" name:

> The LORD, the LORD, the compassionate and gracious God, slow to anger, abounding in love and faithfulness, maintaining love to thousands, and forgiving wickedness, rebellion and sin. Yet he does not leave the guilty unpunished; he punishes the children and their children for the sin of the fathers to the third and fourth generation.

Do you reflect this glorious name in your life? In what ways are you compassionate, gracious, patient, loving, forgiving, and holy? A theology of the "name" leads to intentional practice of that name's significance in personal life.

While God's name inherently denotes His independent and eternal existence, it also connotes His relationship to His people. His consistency in unconditional love and punitive judgment, evokes both joy and dread. Just because I receive His forgiveness for my sin doesn't mean sin will go unpunished. Pardoning and punishing are part of God's name. This great name should be exalted above the earth by humans. It is already excellent in the realm of creation.

Making God look great to humanity is part of reflecting God's glory as His highest purpose for us. For Christians, of course, it is the name of Jesus that we exalt and proclaim in order to make God's name known on the earth. How excellent is *Jesus'* name in all the earth! When Jesus unequivocally claimed greatness over Abraham (John 8:58) as the eternally existing one, He used God's self-defined identity (cf. Ex. 3:14). He said, "I am." It is no wonder that Peter declared Jesus as the only *name* under heaven given among men by which we must be saved (Acts 4:12). The range of meaning of the Old Testament name(s) of God was extended to Jesus. Jesus was the unique and exclusive YHWH,[3] whose name we must believe and reflect on the earth.

Psalm 8 connects with Acts 4 to create a strong argument for Christ's deity and exclusivity. The glorious name of Jesus is to be declared in all the earth. In addition to an inner likeness to this character that pleases Him, an Intentional Life carries an outer expression of the name of Jesus, in witness, evangelism, and proclamation. In both Exodus 33–34 and John 8, the glory of God is in view with His name.

If God Himself proclaims His name, we must proclaim His name. If God Himself proclaims His name to humans, we must proclaim His name to humans. We honor Him through imitation. We promote Him by following His prescriptions. If God Himself proclaims His name to humans in all the earth, we must proclaim His name to humans in all the earth.

We can meditate on His name in quietness, but should never restrict God's name and character to private domain. We should not become seclusive with His name or reclusive in our outlook. Notice how the words "name," "proclaim," and "glory" appear in the original "Ode to Joy":

Sing to the L<small>ORD</small>, *praise his* **name;**

Proclaim *his salvation day after day.*

Declare *his* **glory** *among the nations.*

(Ps. 96:2–3, emphasis mine)

Think for a moment about the implications of this Old Testament version of our glorious commission. We not only see the concepts of God's *intrinsic* glory and *ascribed* glory. There is also a *declared* glory—to be declared by us! If He alone is who He is, then it makes sense that all the earth and creation recognize Him. It also makes sense that all people recognize Him.

What new obedience can you draw from this exhaustive, ulterior purpose for all reality—cosmic, earth, and human creation? Be elaborate and thoughtful. Use the back sheets of this book. Or start a notebook dedicated to God's glory, to explore ways to make Him look great through all areas of your life.

This imperative to make God look great simply brings to the surface what is already there and should be true of our lives. We've managed to submerge the glory of God. Instead, focus life on God's glory, whether you eat, drink, think, speak, or whatever. You'll never go wrong with this focus. If you simply *are*, you simply exist and do nothing else, concentrating on this sole purpose will keep you fulfilled, satisfied, and content. Your focus is absolute. It is absolutely right. It fulfills the New Testament call to do everything—even mundane eating and drinking—to the glory of God (1 Cor. 10:31).

Soul Mission

"Help Wanted" read the large letters on the sign on the office window. Smaller characters continued the advertisement: "Must type 70 words a minute. Must be computer literate. Must be bilingual. An equal opportunity employer."

A dog ambling down the street saw the sign, walked in, and applied for the job.

> *Life without a mission is a tremendous omission.*
>
> 🙚AUTHOR UNKNOWN

The office manager said, "I can't hire a dog for this job."

The dog pointed to the line, "An equal opportunity employer."

The manager said, "Take this letter and type it."

The dog went off to the computer and returned a minute later with the finished letter, perfectly typed.

The manager said, "Here's a problem. Write a computer program for it and run it."

Fifteen minutes later, the dog came back with the correct answer.

The manager still wasn't convinced. "But I can't hire a dog for this position," he said. "You've got to be bilingual."

The dog looked up at the manager and said, "Meow."[1]

Since we started this Intentional Life trilogy by illustrating random animal existence (see Book One, chapter one), I indulge here in a pet philosophical quest to distinguish animals from humans. I cringe when I hear that animals and humans stand in a straight-line continuum; or that animal behavior is not different from human behavior; or that notions of right and wrong are part of our animal heritage. The way some humans act, this view is least complimentary to animals. I wonder if they feel chagrined over our claims to their ancestry, but the fact that our supposed forefathers don't know that they don't know, may verify my observation. If they knew as little as we do, they would never claim to have spawned a monster progeny named "man."

Here are a few distinctions between humans and animals (even though some humans echo orangutan behavior):

➤ *Animals attack, but don't sense injustice or lobby for "fairness."* Some time ago our then eleven-year-old son accused me of unfairness. The next day he sulked all day long. Our dog does not gripe over a grudge.

➤ *Animals exhibit hierarchy, but don't act snobbish. Sibling rivalry seems absent.* They don't look down on neighbors who keep uncut yards. They don't pursue cosmetic makeovers. They don't even brush their teeth. (Perhaps there is a connection here between junior high kids and animal heritage after all!)

➤ *Animals bond to each other, but don't intentionally die for another.* If "survival of the fittest" rules in animal domain, then love takes a beating. There is no martyrdom in animaldom.

➤ *Animals display macro-specie differences.* Humans are a single species. Even physical differences between individuals and races are minimal. Animals can't naturally interbreed between species. In the cat family, we don't have unnatural *tigons* or *ligers,* (tiger-lion). The physical differences within the human species amount to little compared to the huge differences between the same animal species. There are not several kind of species among humans. Humans interbreed across discernible racial and ethnic lines and produce robust children. Unfortunately for the beasts who have no choice, some perverted humans sexually cohabit with some animals. But can a human and a dog crossbreed? Why don't we see caucasoid-terrier *humogs* or real-life mermaids?

➤ *Animals cannot create language.* Humans not only exhibit the ability and use of language, they keep on creating new sentences within limited rules of grammar and vocabulary. By the way, babies all over the world grasp language about the same age. And then there is the phenomena of interlingual learning and communication. Though thousands of spoken languages exhibit widely differing characteristics, they can all be learned by people not born into those groups.

➤ *Animals are not self-conscious.* Pink-bottomed baboons don't feel shame at their open nakedness or mating routines. We called our dog "Fudge" because he is golden-chocolate brown. But he doesn't know himself to be "Fudge," distinguishable as "Fudge" from our neighbor's dog, whose name I presently forget. (But the neighbor's dog doesn't care that I forgot its name; its owner may.) I do mind if a person doesn't care enough to ask how to rightly pronounce my unfamiliar name.[2] I can tell if you have forgotten my name. I wonder if you really remember me. Our dog doesn't know if I addressed him as "stupid" in affection or anger.

➤ *Animals do not discipline their kids anywhere in the world.* My children would like that.

➤ *Animals do not formalize marriage, maintain myths, pass on tradition, make music, worship ancestors, create religions, or conduct last rites for the dead.*

➤ *Animals do not knowingly get stuck in good or bad habits.* They may be trained to relearn habits. But they don't easily lapse into old habits and certainly don't intentionally teach themselves new habits. I saw an advertisement accompanying a woe-struck female face that stated: "I saw a dog and thought: *If I was a dog, I wouldn't have a heroin habit.* I wish I was a dog."[3]

➤ *Animals do not exhibit intentionality in passion, mission, and vision.* They are not capable of intentional action toward an ultimate purpose and personal mission.

After an hour-long campus presentation on belief differences between religions, I was bombarded with questions from inquiring minds. Most questions were neither theoretical nor philosophically oriented, as expected on a provocative subject. They were pragmatic, relating to life, this life. Those students were clearly on a searing search for the purpose of this life. The pragmatic test for truth and trust became the critical issue of which religion best addressed the question of meaning and purpose of life. It takes human, abstract rationality to exhibit voluntary passion and intentional activity toward a mission. Animals don't pursue the "purpose" question.

The best explanations for the biogenetic similarities and nonbiological dissimilarities between animals and humans flow from creaturehood, coming from the same hand of the genius Creator, the Designer-Mind of the universe. Fashioned to exist in the same environment, we share many similar features and physical processes. But the absolute difference between humans and animals is that only humans ask, "What makes us different?" Animals don't wonder, "Why did one primate species, naked, puny, and vulnerable manage to subordinate all the rest and to make this world, and others, its domain?"[4]

People ask the questions: Why did the Maker create humanity? Why were humans put on the earth? Let me put that question straightforwardly: Why are you still left here? Or crudely: Why haven't you died yet?

You've probably asked similar questions. Hopefully your friends aren't wishing you a premature death by asking "Why are you still here, alive, on the earth?" But they don't have to, because that question hovers on the edges of your own consciousness every day. It is a pivotal question for life, reflection, and activity. It is a question about

purpose,

meaning,

direction,

affirmation,

justification, and

commission

and is really a question that determines your mission.

Intentional, not instinctual, passion(s) and mission(s) distinguish humanity from the rest of biology. The first verses of

Psalm 8 set God's mission, the sole mission for human beings, in the context of His glorious creation. As we consider the rest of Psalm 8, we will focus on "soul mission"—a distinctive of humanness. The glory of God is already celebrated in the cosmos. Will it be consummated in humanity?

WHAT IS THE HUMAN RACE?

Psalm 8 bristles with implications of God's ulterior purpose for humanity, the general purpose for existence. Together let's discover the first-floor purpose, the ground-floor reason for all human existence. This psalm will present an articulate summary of our personal mission.

In verses 3–8 the psalmist differentiates human from nonhuman creation in order to elicit God's glory from humankind. The unhesitant reflection of God's glory in nature highlights the precarious choices we make to withhold our recognition of the Creator. "Making God look great" must not only serve as the objective purpose of the human race; it must become the *personal* mission of individual human beings in all of life's dimensions.

Overwhelmed with wonder, the psalmist asks, "What is man?" (8:4; the collective noun "man" may be translated "the human race" or "mortals"). Compared to the universe, human beings are insignificant (vv. 3–4). It takes not wisdom but humility to see that the universe is a magnificent masterpiece of God.

When I consider your heavens,

  the work of your fingers,

the moon and the stars,

  which you have set in place.

One starry night, King David left the stresses of his royal vocation, his electronic organizer, and e-mail inbox and decided to contemplate the heavens instead. You can't do that in most cities today. It's almost impossible to consider the heavens through smog and haze. I suggest you get away and do it sometime. Travel to a place where the cloud cover and light pollution don't obliterate the night skies. Lie on your back and count the stars—on a clear night you can count up to 4,000 (up to 6,000 from a remote location) with the naked eye. First count, then consider and contemplate them. You will inevitably be pointed to their Maker.

All the psalmist knew from a human perspective was pre-scientific astronomy—perhaps science as science is always *pre*-scientific! He reached several significant conclusions. He observed *regularity* in the heavens. The sun rose and set like clockwork. The moon and the stars were regular as well. In the late 1970s and early 1980s, before the days of airline deregulation in the U.S., Allegheny and Braniff were prominent airlines. As rules and competition heated up, these two companies became notorious for cancelled and late flights. In their waning days, a wag suggested that they merge into a new airline, ALL-BRAN, "for then the flights would be regular." The heavenly bodies are always regular.

The psalmist also observed *uniformity* in nature. The sun rises in the east every day. The moon is the same shade—not red today, green tomorrow, and purple the next day. Thrilled with his observation of regularity and uniformity—two fundamental, nonscientific assumptions of all science—he pointed us to the Owner, Maker, and Ruler of creation. These are *Your* heavens (Owner), the work of *Your* fingers (Maker), the moon and the stars which *You* have set in place (Ruler). The LORD-Lord (v. 1) owns, made, and rules over all creation.

Evangelist Billy Graham's long-time associate and soloist, George Beverly Shea, used to sing a wonderful hymn called "It Took a Miracle" (by J.W. Peterson): "My Father is omnipotent, and that you can't deny; the God of might and miracles, 'tis written in the sky. It took a miracle to put the stars in place; it took a miracle to put the world in space." I once heard an American child sing an unfortunate misunderstanding of that lyric: "It took America to put the stars in place; it took America to put the world in space!" The Lord who made them and thus owns them is the One who set them in place.

America and the world know much more about God's heavens from present exploration than King David or Buckminster Fuller or Arthur Clarke dreamed of in sci-fi fantasies. The universe extends in all directions as far as astronomers can see with the most powerful space, optical, and radio telescopes. Our life-sustaining sun is one star of an estimated 200 billion stars (and the star count is still on!). As mentioned earlier, our exquisite but petite Milky Way galaxy is one of 50 to 125 billion (add 11 zeros) guesstimated galaxies, flying through space at a million miles per hour, apparently in the gravitational grip of some hitherto unknown giant mass.[5]

I bring up these enormities for the sake of presently known human proportion, as well as often unrecognized, divine supervision. Whether you want to scale your map of the universe to fit a dining table or a wall, the cosmos runs off the map. All this disproportionate immoderation is God's *finger*work. I want you to imagine the ultimate prodigy, God, and then extrapolate into infinity. Creating this universe was kid's stuff, child's play, like putting together a baby's toy. Creation was simple and easy for God—His *finger*work.

God, of course, doesn't feature human projectiles—fingers. Every time the phrase "the work of your fingers" occurs in the Bible, it poetically refers to a powerful, personal communication of God to human beings. Frustrated Egyptian magicians declared, "This is the finger of God" when they couldn't reproduce the gnat plague unleashed by Moses and Aaron (Ex. 8:19). In that event, Israel's God communicated His rout of an Egyptian deity. The Ten Commandments were inscribed by "the finger of God" (Ex. 31:18)—an articulate communication of His expectations of His people. During his final party, Babylonian king Belshazzar saw some divine finger graffiti (Dan. 5:5–6). To paraphrase God's wall-memo, the divine finger wrote, "The fat lady has sung, the party is over; in fact, Belshazzar's days are numbered. Bye-bye, Babylon, bye-bye. The kingdom and the civilization are finished" (Dan. 5:26–28). Jesus drove out the demons by the finger of God, not by Beelzebub (Luke 11:19–20).

Since haughty-headed humans are hard-hearted, God will pursue anything to get His message through to us. Will we recognize Him for who He is? When humans and God's fingerwork collide, we must recognize God's glory, power, and truth, or suffer the consequences. The psalmist saw creation as God's fingerwork, easy for Him to do, and clear for us to comprehend. The magnificent masterpiece of creation points to its Maker, Owner, and Ruler. Or, as someone quipped, "If there was a Big Bang, there had to be a Big Banger."

Humans are miniscule in terms of the universe. Though insignificant in comparison to the great universe, human beings experience the care of God:

What is man that you are mindful of him,

the son of man that you care for him? (Ps. 8:4)

The psalmist declares, "LORD-Lord, I am awestruck by Your work in creation; but more than that I am moonstruck by Your care for us." He wonders, "What is feeble, weak, mortal man that You are mindful of him?"

Human beings are insignificant in at least two ways when compared to the marvelous majesty of the universe: (1) in size (none 10 feet tall as yet); and (2) in weight (none 1000 pounds heavy, at least not yet), if not in complexity. We are pygmies, dwarfs, undersized, dainty little urchins. In age (not many reach over 150 years anymore, but perhaps in the future) we are insignificant, if not in accomplishment.

However, there is something special about this Lilliputian being: God cares for humans. God remembers, moves, and acts on our behalf. In God's eyes we possess supreme value. Fortunately, God doesn't think bigger is better. We are creatures of worth.

Mary, who worked for the Alaska Department of Corrections, sat between her boyfriend and me on a flight to Singapore. International flights provide opportunities for lengthy conversation, especially during mealtimes. She subscribed to a not-so-bad view of human badness, but then blurted out that "man is nothing more than one of the *gases* in the universe." She, a self-proclaimed gas, was enforcing prison terms on gases sentenced by other gases. Apparently these humans were conscious but purposeless gas. Finally I remarked, "Mary, humanity seems to be the only gas that wonders if it is merely gas. Humanity has to be more than gas to wonder if it is gas at all. Humans have to be more than gas to be criminally charged. In fact, here are two gases, you and me, discussing a nongaseous proposition, that humans are gases." She agreed with the tension and replied, "Perhaps humans commit crime because as gases they don't have pur-ose in life." She understood some of the implications of her position but probably didn't realize how much it called her own existence into question. The "gas" view of human beings provides no purpose to life.

The psalmist ponders God's care for us—more gassers than gases. Indeed we must be more than gases if God cares. Sometime ago a seventeen-year-old friend gassed himself to death. I mourned. I wished I had had the opportunity to convince him of God's care for him. He hadn't believed that truth. God focuses His care on you. Perhaps you feel jailed in a maze where exit signs are hopeless jokes by a cruel jail superintendent. Even the redemption slips are signed by supervisors who don't have signing rights. They too seem to be waiting to die. Instead, the Bible communicates God's fond, inexplicable care for you.

You must be some Thing, for God cares for you.

You must be some Thing unique, for God cares for you.

Therefore, you must be and become some Thing. No situation in life is too desperate to give up on living.

On the other hand, think through the real life implications of the next chain of concepts. If God doesn't exist, He can't care. If God doesn't care, He can't care for you. If God doesn't care for you, there is no ultimate point in living. If there is no ultimate point in living, you can't pursue an ulterior purpose for life. If there is no ulterior purpose to be found, there is no necessary meaning to life. If there is no necessary meaning to life, there is no true life. Only existence exists!

Look at that middle connection again. *If there is no God to care for you, there is no ultimate point, there is no ulterior purpose, and there is no necessary meaning to life.*

This is why God grounds His grand purpose for human living in God's care for human life. Each of us is some Thing, and is some Thing unique—all propositions found in the declared fact that God cares for each of us.

You are valuable, infinitely valuable. It is no wonder that God loves you, gave His irreplaceable Son for you (John 3:16), and bought you with the infinite price of His Son's blood (1 Peter 1:18–19). You are worth more than many sparrows (Matt. 10:31). God cares for you. That truth alone would get me out of bed on some days. The Creator has also made us with purpose in mind. That too should get me out of bed on many days. Paul argues that God bought us at an incredible price so we could make Him look good (1 Cor. 6:20). Therefore, God is for me. Now that should get me out of bed every day, any day! Midget man is majestic in a mighty way. God is for us (Rom. 8:31). We are here to make Him look great in and through our lives.

WHAT THE HUMAN RACE IS

Contrasted with the rest of God's creation, human beings are most important (Ps. 8:5–8). Humanity is most important by rank, recognition, and responsibility.

Man is important by rank. "You made him a little lower than the heavenly beings" (v. 5). "Heavenly beings" is the NIV translation for *elohim*, a frequent word used for "God" in the Old Testament. Since it is plural in form, it is sometimes used to portray the creatures of heaven as higher than humans. The better translation here should read: "God has made humans a little lower than Himself."

Man is spoken of as a "made" creature. He is not the chance offspring of a random mutation in the biological sphere. Mere natural forces do not fortuitously explain his origins or existence. Man's "made-ness" dispels macro-evolutionism.

Since man is a made creature, he is not God. He is different from deity. He is not a part of God. He comes from the hand of God. He can never be or become God, for God can never come to be. Since man is made, he should never be worshipped. Man is not gifted with or capable of divinity.

If God is Number One in the universe, who is now Number Two? Guess who? Human beings. Yet throughout biblical history, Number Two attempts to usurp Number One. That happened in Lucifer's story. It happened in the human story. It also happens in my own story. The problem is that there is and can be only *one* Number One, or else the Number One rank will be unintelligible. The human race has been endowed Number Two status.

God has made humans a little lower than Himself. Contemporary mythology says we are accidentally a little higher than the animals, later and higher in an evolutionary line. Yet Psalm 8:5–8 clearly recalls Genesis 1:26–28. In God's creative activity, He placed man at the height of the earthly realm. We are not a little higher than the earth; we are a little lower than heaven. We are not a little higher than the animals; we are a little lower than the angels. We are not a little higher than nature; we are a little lower than God Himself. Therefore, we rank higher than the earth and all that is in it.

Earlier we said that animals and humans share biological similarities and even some psychological connections. But that doesn't mean we are in an existential or developmental straight line of evolutionary development. Man carries the image or likeness of God (Gen. 1:26–27; 5:1; cf. James 3:9) which animals do not.[6] The primary difference between humans and nonhumans lies in the image of God. Animals don't carry religious sensibility. They do not experience the numinous, the *mysterium tremendum,* the "idea of the holy." According to Psalm 8, the personality difference between you and God is much less than the personality difference between you and your dog, even though you may act like your dog. Man is not an upgraded version of an animal. He was to be the earthly re-presentation of God himself.

We must personally dip into the Number Two rank of humanity. So act your rank. Salute Number One—God. Rule over Number Three—creation.

The human race is important by divine recognition. In a stunning development we discover that the One who gives us being also gives us place and prestige. Psalm 8:5 reads, *"and crowned him with glory and honor."* Unlike animals, man has been crowned, God has shared His glory and honor with man, the midget. A royal display about humanity arises in God's creation intention.

The implications of such human royalty are enormous. For instance, the love and respect of neighbor builds on the premise that humans are different than animals. Urgent salvage efforts are undertaken when a plane crash sends people to a watery grave or leaves them in an unrecognizable condition in the World Trade Center collapses. We don't usually salvage the dead bodies of animals. We attempt to recover what we can of human remains. We feel a critical need to identify them through dental records and fingerprints, even though their bodies were blown apart. We feel a need to bring closure to their earthly existence by giving them a proper funeral. We pay *final respects* to a creature that deserves final respects. A thoroughbred horse in a burning barn is put down. Yet when a scoundrel of a man is caught in a burning house, we attempt to rescue him. Why? The depraved man carries vestiges of God's glory and honor; the racehorse, even if it won the Kentucky Derby, does not.

Ethicists pontificate on the necessity of courtesy, nicety, and respectful conduct toward all people. We dare to probe them for the foundation of that ethical stance. If man is made in the image of God and carries the remains of creation glory and honor, then it does matter that we are sociable, kind, and create systems to protect his respect. However, if a man came from nothing or no thing, he can be treated like nothing or no thing. If a man descended from animal heritage, he should be treated as an animal. Put him down at the slightest hint of suffering. We wouldn't need to wonder at the snuffing out of pre-natal life or post-active life by painless medical procedures. If man is the result of a cosmic accident, his body need not be salvaged, accidents need not be studied to prevent future ones, because everything is an accident. If you are a germ growing up to be a worm, we don't have to care if you squirm.

However, in a biblical view of the human race when we demean man, we demean God. We rob God's glory and honor from human life. We care for fragile humans, the dis-enfranchised, the suffering poor, because vestiges of the divine image, glory, and honor remain in all humans. They are not carriers of divinity; they are carriers of *dignity*. We respect God by respecting man. Can I get humanity some respect? "Love thy neighbor." A disgruntled stockholder walked into the office and bellowed: "Anybody with a little authority here? I want to talk to someone with a little authority around here." He was directed to the president's office, with the added remark, "The Chief Executive has as little authority as anyone else around here!" By contrast, when we love our neighbor, we are acting under God's authority and making Him look good.

UNDER GOD, OVER NATURE

Back to Psalm 8. Look at how verses 6–8 explain the responsibility that flows from man's rank and recognition in the classification of life:

You made him ruler over the works of your hands;

> *you put everything under his feet;*

all flocks and herds,

> *and the beasts of the field*

the birds of the air,

> *and the fish of the sea,*

> *all that swim the paths of the seas.*

The psalmist discerns a distinct hierarchy of authority and responsibility in nature. Man is Number Two. All the other works of God's hands, including plant and animal life, are Number Three. Now Number Three challenges Number Two, even as Number Two disregards the Number One position. God has made man ruler over the works of God's hands.

Natural disasters remind man that he is at the mercy of nature—its laws, its powers, its unpredictability. Over recent years, summer droughts in Texas resulted in scorched grass, brown pastureland, and parched earth—one of the worst natural disasters in the state's history. The place was bone-dry. Cattle prices and land prices fell, but rural humor rose to the occasion. Ranchers were heard discussing the benefits of moving to hell, because "that would be an improvement." Meanwhile, the cows were giving evaporated milk, weeping willows couldn't, and farmers who chewed had to prime themselves to spit. One man even saw two trees fighting over a dog. Pete the rancher "droughted out" in the 1950s, opened up a hardware store and sold hammers for $1.00, a dollar less than wholesale. Yes, he lost a dollar each time he sold a hammer, he explained, but it sure beat ranching! Drought decimated Texas, yet floods drowned the Midwest at the same time. Earthquakes in China, floods in Bangladesh, famine in Ethiopia, and cyclones in the Philippines put people at the mercy of fickle nature.

According to Psalm 8, however, human beings are placed over nature in rulership even though nature is more powerful than they. Here is the grid for the Creator's intent, the human mission, in revelation and nature:

> Man is master and manager, but never the Maker.

> Man is subduer and steward, but never the Sovereign.

Man is subduer and master, delegated as ruler over nature. God has put everything under his feet. In contemporary religion there is a return to Mother Nature, Brother Gorilla, and Sister Tomato. Sedona, Arizona, one of the most beautiful places on earth, supposedly features a "vortex of divine energy" according to New Agers. In cultural anthropology films I have seen nature worshipers going around in worship circles bowing to awe-evoking nature. I thought only preliterary cultures worshiped nature. I found it that lay outside Sedona—but these places are never too far to access from driveable highways!

Awe-inspiring nature generates religious sentiment. Nature is impressive, beautiful, and evocative. It brings on feelings of smallness, humility, and joy. It is no wonder that nature has replaced God, since He is said to have "died" in the early part of the twentieth century and been buried around mid-century. In the vacuum, we considered humans as possible candidates for worship but quickly gave up on them. They intentionally maimed and killed each other. That left nature as the only contestant left that was worship-able. So we've come full circle back to nature religion—primitive religion.

According to a Judeo-Christian view of natural reality, man is placed over nature as subduer and master. Nature has no human qualities. Neither does it have divine qualities. We don't have to worry about emptying nature of divinity or humanity, because it evidences neither. Creation was given to man by God to subdue it and master it. Humanity retains preeminence over other creatures in value and function. This role was part of God's original purpose for human kind.

My family visited Mount St. Helens fifteen years after a violent volcano decimated that region. As we came to the crest of the mountain, we suddenly felt like we were attending a funeral for our earthly residence. Entire forests still looked like toothpicks spilled on a summer picnic table, sparse and random in formation. But the efforts of the U.S. Forest Service in nursing the area are bringing a revival to this part of our country. An occasional green tree juts out of the rock. Flowers are beginning to show up again. Hurrah to the nature ruler, the dominion haver, creation's caretaker.

Generally speaking, man has exercised dominion over animals from the earliest times. He tamed wolves, called them dogs, and has enjoyed them ever since as pets. Cats, though, seem impervious to taming and insist on adopting humans as pets. Internet humor reads, "Dogs answer the phone; cats ask you to take a message!" Wild oxen were trained to carry loads; camels to walk across the desert; elephants to haul cargo; doves to carry mail; parrots to communicate. "All kinds of animals, birds, reptiles and creatures

of the sea are being tamed and have been tamed by man"
(James 3:7). Zoos prove our fascination with the wild kingdom. Circuses prove our ability to tame and train animals.
"Dominion-having" could allow man to bring creation to
full bloom.

Unfortunately, instead of wisely ruling nature, man often
seems intent on recklessly ravishing nature. When they yield
to the immorality of the Fall by exercising insensitivity and
acquisition, humans harass nature instead of harnessing it.
Number 2 attempts to obliterate Number 3 as well as other
Number 2s and makes a statement against Number 1. So we
need the other half of the biblical couplet on man's responsibility to nature.

Man is to be steward and manager. Man is to subdue the
earth, but he is not to play sovereign over it. Man is to be
master of nature, but he does not possess the Maker's rights
over it. Psalm 8:5 reads, *You made him*. Man does not own
independent rights over the earth. He carries delegated
rights. When Number Two plays Number One as owner,
ruler, and maker, he will rape and abuse nature. He will even
go to the extent of abusing and raping other *humans*.
Economic history in slave trading and sweat-shop labor
reveals that inclination. Daily news confirms the bad news.
Man often doesn't care for the future of other humans who
need a human-friendly home to live. Man does not retain
absolute, independent control of nature. He doesn't sit in
God's place over nature. Neither does he sit in nature's place.
He must know what his place is and use it rightly.

Intellectuals these days proclaim a new paradigm of reality. Galileo de-centered the *earth* when he proposed that we
lived in a heliocentric universe. His correction shattered the
supposed biblical paradigm of the supposed gullible, Bible-

believing Middle Ages. Of course the Bible nowhere says that the earth is the geographical center of the universe. It simply holds the earth to be the redemptive center of the universe. Contemporary thinkers say we need to de-center *humanity* as the focus of the earth. The Bible does say that man is under God over nature. Sometimes we position ourselves above God (classical, secular humanism), and at other times we position ourselves inside God and under nature (classical monistic pantheism). Biblically speaking, we remain under God over nature.

This is why Psalm 8 ends the same way it begins. It does not end with, "O MAN, our man, how majestic is your name in all the earth!" It is not, "O NATURE, our nature, how majestic is your name in all the earth!" It is, "O LORD, our Lord, how majestic is your name in all the earth!" (v. 9). For as man fulfills his original purpose from God on the earth, God is glorified. As man fulfills God's creative intent, God looks good.

MAKE GOD LOOK

Psalm 8 is quoted in the New Testament as finding fulfill-ment in the Second Man, the Last Adam, the Lord Jesus Christ. In His incarnation (Heb. 2) and His eventual ruler-ship of this earth (cf. 1 Cor. 15:35–49; Eph. 1:22), Jesus reestablishes what humanity was supposed to be. God has put all things under His feet. Jesus is the Man for all mankind, from the first to the last of all humanity. He is the example of all examples for all who need an example to fol-low. Eventually, those who have put their trust in Him will become like Him and function like Him.

How? Notice the possessive pronoun, "O LORD, *our* Lord." The Creator God of glory can be our own covenant

God of salvation. In this way, all our small accomplishments can shine, share, show-off His splendor to the world. By relating to Him as our God, He pervades our fallen human-ness and earthbound clay-ness, and restores us to visibly display the glory of the invisible God.

Therefore, whatever you do, do all to the glory of God. Make God's glory your soul's sole purpose, your ulterior mission. Make God look good in all your roles, relationships, and responsibilities. For example:

➤ *In your family,*

If you are a parent, be the best parent you can be, displaying God's glory to your children.

If you are a teenager, you are to carry the honor of God in your home, school, and relationships.

If you are a housewife, God values your role in the family. Make God look good there.

➤ *In your vocation,*

If you are a teacher, you are to be the best teacher you can be, for you are a royal display of God's glory.

If you are a doctor, you must be the best you can be, for you are wearing God's dignity in your surgical attire.

If you are an engineer, businessman, plumber, secretary, mechanic, writer, accountant, whatever you do, do all to the glory of God.

Make God look . . . great! Through you. Today, tomorrow, for a lifetime. This is our human mission extended and derived from our spiritual passion. Every endeavor must ultimately be judged by whether or not it is an appropriate submission or mission component of our ultimate purpose. Making God look great is humanity's sole mission that must be personalized and translated into our own soul mission.

CHAPTER

Theologizing Life

A sniper bullet landed in the bunker. The visiting commanding officer hastily ordered his soldiers to get rid of the offending sniper right away. A sergeant gently informed him that the sniper had actually been at it for the last six days and was rather inaccurate in his shots. They preferred to leave him in place, for if they got rid of him, he might be replaced with a far more accurate sniper!

God has created you for consistent application of life's mission to make Him look great. Often you may pursue the mission arbitrarily, hitting the target by chance rather than skill or intention. Like the bad sniper, the enemy loves to have you stay in

> *We have lived to see a time without order*
> *In which everyone is confused in his mind,*
> *One cannot bear to join in the madness,*
> *But if he does not do so*
> *He will not share in the spoils,*
> *And will starve as a result.*
> *Yes, God; wrong is wrong;*
> *Happy are those who forget,*
> *Happier yet those who remember and have deep insight.*
> ❧CLASSICAL JAVANESE POEM

place because you are seldom accomplishing God's mission for your life. You occasionally and accidentally stray into the mission of God's glory. Generally, though, you are a pretender on the mission. I challenge you to overhaul, restructure, and organize your life around God's glory. "Happier yet," ends our judicious opening poem from Indonesia above, "those who remember and have deep insight."

You need to carry deep insight about two truths: *mortality* and *greatness* are both inscribed on your life. Finitude and the divine image characterize your existence. You are weak and feeble, unable to contribute to the mission, so you need to be sustained by God.

On mortality, feebleness, and finitude, God's Word says:

➤ You will not exist on the earth for long. You are not as important as you think you are (James 4:14).

➤ You are negligible, disposable, discardable—dust (Genesis 3:19).

➤ You are a maggot, an insignificant worm (Job 25:6).

➤ You are a grasshopper to God—trivial and minor (Isa. 40:22). Grasshoppers have five sets of eyes, but cannot look up. And up is where God is.

Humans are diminutive and immaterial in the comparative status of things. You've got to remember your relative insignificance against the size and age of the universe. You shouldn't flirt with God's Number One rank. You cannot be proud. You must learn to look up even though you are like a grasshopper.

However, if you set your life to it, you can make a specific, unique, vital contribution to God's glory on the earth. Your fleeting appearance in history can mean and amount to something. You can be an intentional and joyful participant in God's purposes!

The life that you intentionally build on the foundation of godly passion will extend into mission. The passion will testify to your heartbeat and the mission will testify to your lifestyle. You can carry out the mission *of* your life *in* your life. Indeed, God has bestowed Number Two ranking on you—the perfect place for a unique creation to make Him look great.

In truth, the worlds were created for you

to enjoy, discover, and develop as you relate to nature,

to be the arena where you represent God,

to make God look good. To reveal His honor. To receive His revelation. To reflect His character.

"A man should carry two stones in his pocket," goes a Middle Eastern proverb. "On one should be inscribed, 'I am but dust and ashes.' On the other: 'For my sake was the world created.' And he should use each stone as he needs its reminder." Yet just because every life is special does not mean every life is strategic. You can intentionally receive and reflect God's glory through your life.

A THEOLOGY OF "GLORY"

I would like to lead you through a quick Bible study on "glory" as human mission, and then apply a theology of glory from the New Testament to your life as your *personal* mission. We will theologize your life, much as one would "winterize" a car, in order to get you ready for the next season of your life—the rest of your life. All through the New Testament human beings are prodded to glorify God.

First, the people who fill its pages move us by example to glorify God. Note the following sampling.

➤ The shepherds at the birth of Jesus threw a party to

God's glory (Luke 2:20). Anyone who would listen and everyone who would see could sense God's glory.

➤ Glory to God accompanied Jesus' healings (Matt. 15:31; Mark 2:12; Luke 7:16). Both beneficiary and observer were often drawn to give God glory.

➤ Jesus' glory and the Father's glory share an inseparable spotlight (John 11:4; 13:31; 17:5; Heb. 1:3).

➤ Jesus explained His earthly purpose as a mission to glorify the Father by His work (John 17:4).

➤ Jesus prayed to the Father to glorify Him (John 17:1 5) in order that He, in turn, might glorify His Father.

➤ The apostle Paul's gospel proclamation reached more and more people and caused thanksgiving to overflow to the glory of God (2 Cor. 4:15).

Second, several New Testament *events* prompt us to glorify God.

➤ Jesus' transfiguration captured the glory of God (Matt. 17:1–8; cf. 2 Peter 1:17).

➤ Jesus' resurrection placed Him in a position of glory (Eph. 1:20–21).

➤ Jesus presently occupies the position of glory for which human beings were created (Heb. 2:9).

➤ Jesus answers prayer that advances God's work and brings God glory (John 14:13).

➤ Jesus will come in the glory of the Father (Luke 9:26). Every tongue will eventually confess Jesus Christ is Lord, to the glory of the Father (Phil. 2:11).

➤ Jesus' judgment of unbelievers separates them from His presence and glory (Matt. 13:37–43).

➢ Those who don't know God or obey the gospel of our Lord Jesus Christ will be punished with everlasting destruction, shut out from the presence of the Lord and from the majesty of His power on the day He comes to be glorified (2 Thess. 1:9–10). They will never get to glorify Jesus the way God wanted them to. They don't do it now either.

Third, New Testament *eulogies* stimulate glory to the Lord.

➢ God is glorified by nations believing and obeying Him (Rom. 16:26–27). Therefore, we must proclaim Jesus Christ (Rom. 16:25). You may glorify Him for His salvation.

➢ God is glorified by providing for all the needs of the saints according to His glorious riches in Christ Jesus (Phil. 4:19–20). Have you glorified Him for His provision?

➢ God is glorified for the safe spiritual delivery of believers into heaven (2 Tim. 4:18). You will glorify Him for His present and eternal spiritual protection someday. You can start now on this unique "safety" feature of the Christian faith.

Finally, New Testament *exhortations* also bond the believer to the glory of God.

➢ When there is unity among the believers, it results to the glory of the God and Father of our Lord Jesus Christ (Rom. 15:6). We must accept one another, just as Christ accepted us, in order to bring praise to God (Rom. 15:7).

➤ When we are filled with the fruit of righteousness that comes through Jesus Christ—it brings glory and praise of God (Phil. 1:11).

➤ When we live a godly life revealing character and discipleship, sourced in Christ, the Father is glorified (John 15:8).

➤ When we keep ourselves from sexual immorality, we glorify God with our bodies (1 Cor. 6:18–20).

➤ When we indulge in good works, unbelievers will glorify God (Matt. 5:16; 1 Peter 2:12).

➤ When we suffer or are insulted for the name of Christ, we are blessed, for the Spirit of glory and of God rests on us (1 Peter 4:14). We can praise God that we bear Christ's name (1 Peter 4:16).

In diverse ways and repeated strategies, the Scriptures stir Christians to glorify God. The latter part of 2 Peter 1:3, "who called us by his own glory and goodness," could be translated in both ways. God has called us *to* His glory and goodness *and* called us *by* His glory and goodness. Glory shows His perfection and His standard. Fortunately, "His divine power has given us everything we need for life and godliness through our knowledge of him who called us by his own glory and goodness" (2 Peter 1:3).

Let's land this quick New Testament flight into God's glory—His essential purpose, an intrinsic trait, and our ulterior purpose for existence. This wealth of observations calls us to insight and application, to theologize our lives with God's glory—to not only *let* God look good through us, but to *make* God look good through us.

THEOLOGIZE YOUR LIFE

Glory correlates to God's perfections. We are somewhat at a loss to describe the divine excellencies that parallel divine glory. That should be understandable since it points clearly to our human limitation. But we may trust the Bible for guidance here too. Here are six summary expressions of *glory* derived from Scripture, to theologize your life.

1. Glory connects presence with an elevated sense of awareness.

Glory can be ignored, but only with deliberate effort. You've experienced presence. When a "glorious" person walks into a room, everyone takes notice. Conversations cease, drinks settle, heads turn to meet this person who carries presence.

The glory of God's presence demands all human attention. In the Old Testament it is called *shekinah*. Since most of the Old Testament speaks about the transcendence of God, the use of *shekinah* highlights His immanence—His palpable presence among His people. The utter *otherness* of God adds awesomeness to God's nearness. Isaiah 57:15 weds God's distance with proximity, "I live in a high and holy place, but also with him who is contrite and lowly in spirit." Jesus was God's "Immanuel"—*God with us*. The transcendent God became present to us. Christians connect glory with presence. God's glory demands concentration. The Lord Jesus claims focused attention.

Consider the following resolution and questions. Since glory connects with His presence, and since glory inhabits God's earthly dwelling (for example, you can trace this powerful theme from the portable tabernacle beginning in Exodus 40:34-38), and since your body is the equivalent of the Old Testament temple (1 Cor. 6:19)—

In what ways are you giving attention to God's presence in your life?

Are you about God? Are you displaying His glory?

Do your spiritual eyes rise to meet Him?

2. Glory is interchangeable with light.

Shekinah not only refers to presence, but also relates to light—another intrinsic attribute of God. In the New Jerusalem, the "glory of God is its light" (Rev. 21:23). Light floods our activities, dispels darkness, and reveals the hidden. To live for the glory of God trains the divine searchlight on our actions.

To what degree are your activities focused on God's glory? Are you involved in deeds of darkness? What you can't do in the light will not bring glory to God.

3. Glory parallels holiness.

The angels in the heavenly temple sing in poetic, complementary parallelism, "Holy, holy, holy, is the Lord Almighty, the whole earth is full of his glory" (Isa. 6:3; cf. the songs of Rev. 4 and 5). Smoke fills the temple (Isa. 6:4). "Holy smoke" parallels glory. Smoke, glory, and holiness together communicate distance, incomprehensibility, greatness, unapproachability, power, etc. "And the temple was filled with smoke from the glory of God and from his power and no one could enter the temple" (Rev. 15:8).[1] God is far and great. He is glorious.

For a decade I taught a seminary-level spiritual life course (if the spiritual life can be taught in a classroom) in six cycles over a semester. The first cycle began with "glory" and its ramifications, followed by "holiness" and its implications, with the third being "love" and its application. I was able to touch on the cognitive basics of the spiritual life under these headings. I often struggled with putting glory at the helm of the course as the theme of Scripture, when Jesus explicitly affirmed the first commandment of love as the foremost of all. As you noticed in this series, I have made our love for God the underlying purpose, personally *prior* to glorifying God, though the latter is the ulterior purpose of all Christian living. In any case, the three—love of God, glory to God, and holiness in God—can be distinguished but not divided in an integrated view of intentional spirituality.

God's glory could be placed at the peak of the divine triangle. God's purpose for all creation, especially humanity, is His glory. The other points of the triangle designate God's holiness and love. When I ask students for God's essential attribute, they normally vote between "holy" and "love." God's basic attribute is neither of these alone. As I read the Scriptures, His quintessential attribute is hyphenated—*holy-love.*

The angels surround the throne heartily singing the *trisagion*, "Holy, holy, holy" (Isa. 6:3; Rev. 4:8–9). But the first commandment is quadrangular, equal-sided *love* (Mark 12:30; cf. Deut. 6:5). On the hyphen that links "holy" and "love" sits a vertical line to turn it into a symbolic cross, the divine plus sign—holy + love. His holiness separates us from Him. His love reaches out to us. Holy-Love is hyphenated by Jesus, the foundation rock,[2] which God laid (Isa. 28:16; Eph. 2:20; 1 Peter 2:4), Paul preached (1 Cor. 3:11), and from which the people drank (1 Cor. 10:3–4).[3] *Cur Deus Homo!* (Latin for "Why did God become man?") That's why the God-Man. From holy-love flows God's expectations and enablement, His standards and sufficiency, His perfections and His process toward His glory. The more holy a person is, the more glory a person brings to God—the more God's glory becomes apparent in and through that life. To be holy is to be like God. To be like God makes God look good on earth.

How much do you look like God? How separate are you from everything that is not like Him? The more you compromise God's holiness, the less honor you bring to God who has staked His glory among humans around your life.

4. Glory equals power.

The power of God brings glory to God. God's sheer power is revealed in universal creation, human providence, and salvation purpose (see Rom. 1–11), and results in God's glory (Rom. 11:33–36). A glorious God is an all-powerful God, able to bring His plans to completion. "My soul glorifies the Lord" sang Mary (Luke 1:46), because "nothing is impossible with God" (Luke 1:37). God is able to do anything within His character and plans for His glory. Therefore, God must be glorified. God's power proceeds from His glory. The majesty of His power is the glory of His might (2 Thess. 1:9). The unbeliever will be everlastingly excluded from all that God's power can do to bring Himself glory.

When the power of God is demonstrated in your life, you bring glory to Him. Just as creation reveals His eternal power (Rom. 1:20), so does the gospel—the power of God for everyone's salvation (Rom. 1:17). The gospel's claim on you is one of the finest evidences of the glory of God. It is the beginning of the possibility of your intentional display of God's glory. The gospel provides the resources for you to bring God's glory to fruition in your life.

5. Glory accompanies God's goodness in saving humans.

Gospel means "good news." This *good* news is the power of God that brought you salvation and brought Him glory. It is good news because a good God orchestrates the sequence by which you are rescued from the kingdom of darkness and brought into the kingdom of light (Col. 1:13). The divine side of our salvation and godliness integrates God's glory and goodness in His call to our conversion.

> ➤ If God possessed glory only, it would evoke astonishment. I would have to wear "ultraviolet protection" sunglasses all the time. Goodness filters glory.

> ➤ If God possessed holiness only, it would be devastating. I would sit with a motorcycle helmet in my office chair. Goodness filters holiness.

> ➤ If God possessed justice only, I wouldn't have a chance. I would be a fugitive on the run, hoping to hide from heaven. Goodness filters justice.

Divine glory, holiness, and justice stun me. I would submit to God in fear. But all personal faith requires a valid object. The good God is that valid, value-laden object.

The God of the Bible is not just abstractly good; He is absolutely, but *personally* good. He is the highest good for humanity. The Old Testament affirms that His world is good (Gen. 1:18); His word is good (cf. Isa. 39:8); His work is good (Gen. 50:20); His Spirit is good (Ps. 143:10); and His inheritance is good (Prov. 28:10).

The Lord Jesus particularized and standardized goodness in God alone (Matt. 19:17; Mark 10:18; Luke 18:19). Jesus Himself claims to be the good shepherd (John 10:11–14) who lays down His life for His sheep. While no human does good (Rom. 3:12), Christ's goodness transfers to believers (2 Cor. 5:21). Therefore, Christians are to do good (1 Tim. 6:18; Heb. 10:24; 13:16) because they were eternally destined to good works (Eph. 2:10).

So God's goodness and glory are integrated. His goodness is gloriously demonstrated in our salvation (2 Peter 1:3). In our good works, His glory is recognized even by unbelievers (1 Peter 2:12). If God's glory accompanies His goodness, your personal faith for salvation is the platform to gloriously exhibit His goodness. If you have made the critical decision to trust the Lord Jesus alone for your salvation, you will receive His goodness. You will demonstrate His glory.

Further, your good works bring Him glory. Consider your day today. What good will you pursue? Whose good will you seek? Are you doing the good you know ought to be done (James 4:17)? Are you sharing with others and thus pleasing God (Heb. 13:16)? Are you reflecting God's goodness in your life, a goodness that He shows to the just and the unjust (Luke 6:35; cf. Matt. 5:45)? Are you showing the vitality of your faith by your good deeds (James 2:17–26)? Are you commanding the rich to do good (1 Tim. 6:18)? Are you spurring others on to good deeds (Heb. 10:24)? Are people seeing your good deeds and praising your Father who is in heaven (Matt. 5:16)? You will please Him in every way by bearing fruit in every good work (Col. 1:10). Check your heart. Are you strategically responding to these questions?

Finally, since the God of glory is also good, I can love and trust Him. I should imitate His goodness. I must turn from evil and do good.

6. Glory, *in its rudimental sense, translates the Hebrew word for "weight."*

If you study *kabod* (the Hebrew word usually translated *glory*), the lexicons and etymologies will help you discover that *glory* literally means "heavy," and figuratively expresses "honor." Relating the two concepts, you'll find that "the heavy" are to be honored. Even today in impoverished economies, the heavy are honored, because they have the means to buy better and nore food.[4] While people may now look down on fatness in he United States, the physically heavy were honored as late as he Depression Era. There are many pictures of heavyset national leaders because they could imbibe good food while the rest of the nation scrambled for a basic diet.

The physical connotation of glory means heavy (e.g., Lam. 3:7). The social connotation was figurative, meaning "the concept of a '[weighty]' person in society, someone who is honorable, impressive, worthy of respect."[5] Certain credit card companies tout their cards as carrying "weight" around the world. Theologically, "glory" is used of God's self-revelation in the cloud-pillar (Ex. 16:10); devouring fire on Sinai (Ex. 24:16–17; cf. Lev. 9:23–24); the back parts of God's glory that Moses saw (Ex. 33:18–23); His presence in the ark (1 Sam. 4:21–22). "Glory" is also used of the recognition that is due to God and the reputation God conveys in His works of self-manifestation (Ps. 19:1). Since all humans were made for the purpose of glorifying God (Isa. 43:7), they ought to give God the recognition due Him (1 Chron. 16:29). Put the recognition and weight concepts together and you'll discover that God is recognized by those who give Him weight in their lives. The increasing recognition of God in your life receives His increasing weight in your life.

WEIGHT AND MISSION

German atheist Friedrich Nietzsche prophetically uttered a profundity: "When God dies, cultures become weightless." Where God dies, God's weight is absent. Where God's weight is absent, God dies. I take this "weight" of God concept as impinging on, controlling, comprising, and comprehending everything in personal life mission. If God has weight in your life, He will look great through your life.

The mission of life is to glorify God by giving Him weight in all of life's dimensions, since He occupies the position of the only true "heavyweight" around. God must carry the heaviest weight in my life, especially since He can carry the heaviest weight that I lay on Him.

This theological study on God's weight of glory must come to an end while God's inexhaustible glory goes on forever. Human sin curbs our meeting the standard of God's glory (Rom. 3:23), but God's salvation allows us to rejoice in the hope of the glory of God (Rom. 5:2). We reflect God's glory and are being transformed into His (Christ's) likeness with ever-increasing glory (2 Cor. 3:18) till the day comes when we will fulfill Psalm 8 (see chapter 4 and Heb. 2:5–9). We will be fully glorified (Rom. 8:30; note the certainty of a past tense word used of a future event!) to give God the glory fully due to Him. At present, the more we look like Christ, the more we will reflect God's glory (2 Cor. 3:18). This life becomes the present process of glory, our becoming more like Him. Indeed, He has prepared believers in advance for His glory (Rom. 9:23). You will ascend a singular mountain peak, because He transforms you in the process of the climbing expedition.

The strange, just-like-God-thing is God's bequest of glory to those who bring Him glory. Just like Jesus is glorified in bringing glory to the Father, we too are glorified in not embezzling His glory. In some way God shares His resplendence with those who represent Him. God makes people great so He can receive people's glory. As we saw in Psalm 8, God has crowned humanity with glory and honor (v. 5), a crowning that only Jesus fully displays (John 13:31–32; Heb. 2:9). We royal crown wearers carry some of the dignity of God in our lives. Our splendor, of course, does not make us deities. Like the elders of heaven, we cast our crowns back at His feet (Rev. 4:10). This is the only appropriate response to God's glory in eternal heaven and provides the irresistible incentive to let go of our crowns.

The glory of God is the be-all and end-all of the inner life and the Intentional Life. That's why we call it *ulterior* purpose. It is most often hidden but occasionally shows. We are overwhelmed by His glorious character, plan, and works (Rom. 11:33–36). We are afraid and worship His glorious, powerful ability (Ezek. 44:4). We worship His glorious person (Rev. 14:7). We fall prostrate in humility at His magnificence (Rev. 4:10–11; 7:11–12). We are surprised by His incredible mysteries (1 Cor. 2:9–10). With others we exalt Him, worship Him, fall down before Him. "Glorify the Lord with me; let us exalt his name together" (Ps. 34:3). We are abandoned to bringing Him glory in everything we are and do as Christians (1 Cor. 6:20; 10:31). Glory brings cohesion to all the excellencies of God in Himself and in us. We want to carry a single eye toward glorifying the General (cf. 2 Tim. 2:3) who, in divine omniscience, focuses on us. And since this ulterior purpose is about God, it is a good ulterior motive, over and against mistaken ulterior motives that could dominate us.

Nicholas of Cusa, a fifteenth-century prelate, sent his monks a portrait to match his treatise, *De Visione Dei (The Gaze of God)*. "The painting showed simply the all-seeing eye of God. . . . no matter at what angle one looked at it, the eye seemed to be focused singly and lone upon the beholder."[6]

I think about my last twenty-four hours to examine whether my actions brought glory to God, whether they featured the weight of God, and approximated the perfections of God as He beheld my life. The quest brings a holy hush into my soul.

➤ Early yesterday morning I read a devotional selection while on my exercise bike. I was strangely moved, warmed, and filled. Did I combine spiritual and physical fitness to the glory of God?

➤ I hurriedly kissed my wife good-bye, anxious to negotiate a horrific expressway. Would a lingering embrace in farewell have been more to the glory of God?

➤ I worked on a speech to be heard by large numbers of people. Did I feel a need to embellish the sermon just to keep up a reputation for learning and style? Whose reputation was my focus?

➤ My lunch with a colleague was an opportunity to build each other up. That resulted in honoring God.

➤ I took an afternoon phone call, inviting me to another speaking engagement and evoking a condescending spirit in me, since I had already scheduled my quota of small events for that year. I know my silent resistance did not please God.

➤ I listened to a message on my voice mail from an unknown fellow-minister, who introduced himself twice using his title, "Dr. Bob _____." Self-introductions with titles irk me. Will I return his call? I would if I was to give him a chance to introduce himself to me as plain ol' Bob. That would elevate God's honor in my heart. He did later.

➤ Playing basketball with the kids (on a lowered seven-foot pole), taking them swimming, enjoying leftovers, our family band practice, all enhanced God's name. I sense that God-concepts come from father concepts, and it was God-honoring to spend time with my children in ways that parallel God's focus on me.

And so ran my day.

➤ This morning's readings of Psalm 30 and Françoise Fénelon on my exercise bike were rich. Glancing through last Sunday's *New York Times* weekly magazine was interesting.

➤ I hurriedly kissed my wife good-bye to negotiate the horrific expressway again. (I didn't know I would be writing a confession about hurried family farewells.) Tomorrow, she gets lots of kisses, for I want to dignify her. In doing that, I would obey God's commands to love my wife as Christ loved the church and so crown God with glory, honor, power, and wisdom in my life.

➤ Today I watch for opportunities, threats, and temptations as means to make God look good in my responsibilities. To praise Him with my lips. To enthrone Him in my life.

God's greatness is inscribed on my life. God's glory is prescribed for my life. How will I make God look good, reflect the inscription, and obey His prescription? I am abandoned to His will for His glory. Every day my father prays, "God, let me not use You to advance my glory. Instead, use me to advance Your glory." Further, I am lost for words about God's glory. It generates astonishment, awe, acknowledgment, apprehension, and abandonment. Johannes Kepler (1571–1630) reminisced, "I wanted to become a theologian; for a long time I was restless. Now, however, observe how through my efforts God is being celebrated in astronomy."

You've read a fair share of urban legends in my writings already. Here comes one from the annals of preachers about a young violinist playing his first ever concert at a music hall in New York City. He received a standing ovation. As he met guests in the foyer, someone asked him why he didn't make eye contact with the audience while playing. He seemed to be looking up at the second balcony. The violinist replied, "I'm glad you noticed. In that balcony was sitting my violin instructor. I wanted to see him smile more than hear the people clap." That's like living for the pleasure and the glory of God in all aspects of our lives.

Let's honor, promote, and please Him in all we do. Let's theologize life, for the more weight God has *in* my life, the more great He looks *through* my life. And, whatever we are and do, let's pursue the ulterior purpose—to make God look great!

Vectoring Life

The opening of Cincinnati's Aronoff Center in 1996 was heralded as the most important event in decades of American architecture. The A-list of the social elite showed up for the grand occasion. Top architects wore black-tie outfits to the ribbon-cutting ceremonies and dinner. They lauded the designer who

> *You should know that a man of knowledge lives by acting, not by thinking about acting, nor by thinking about what he will think when he has finished acting.*
> *A man of knowledge chooses a path with heart and follows it.*
> ⊠CARLOS CASTAÑEDA, *A SEPARATE REALITY*

"has made a career out of pushing the boundaries of architecture, designing buildings that are deliberately provocative." Architectural students at the College of Design, Art, Architecture and Planning at the University of Cincinnati excitedly dubbed it a "postmodern" building. The structure was designed to represent a philosophy without moorings. It goes every which way. "Its form is sharply angled, with few of its walls perpendicular to the floors; from the outside many walls lean outward, and the whole building looks rather as if it had been frozen after the first shocks of an earthquake."[1]

Of course, we know that the building's foundation was not arbitrarily constructed. We are confident that construction materials were not haphazardly compounded. A myriad of codes (electrical, plumbing, structural) received meticulous attention to pass inspections. The "provocative" exterior turns out to be a rather superficial attempt to hide and deny highly integrated and necessary internal systems. Unfortunately, our lives too often look like the Aronoff Center. The salvation foundation has been well laid, but the visible parts of life seem to be put together capriciously. Like that building, we present an unintentional façade to observers.

As with a building or a house, a well-built life also assumes a well-laid foundation with well-mixed materials meeting well-planned codes towards a direction. When we live randomly or, to use biblical terms, live in a fleshy and worldly manner, we resemble that postmodern architectural edifice. Great foundation, but we display the "earthquake look." The life-building process is not vectored rightly, set on intentional missions arising out of our soul mission. An examination of the construction process may give us a clue about where we neglected the divine blueprints:

➤ Salvation laid the foundation for any future building expansion.

➤ The spiritual life continually maintains the foundation in the process of living.

➤ Passion provides the materials and structure for building beyond the basement.

➤ Mission establishes ground-floor purpose.

If your life-building has taken on a wrecked and random appearance, go back to check the construction process you have been following, and see whether you have vectored life toward the mission of your divine Architect.

THE JESUS MODEL

We have said before that we must distinguish between "of" and "in" as crucial modifiers of passion, mission, and vision. In an important sense, we are looking at a process that closely parallels Jesus' incarnation—relating to heaven and earth, God and the world, and the internal and external life. We share the passion/mission/vision "of" life with spiritually growing Christians who are seeking after the same purposes for life—the person, pleasure, and program of God. The passion/mission/vision "in" life connects us to the world—with conscientious nonbelievers and once-saved, carnal Christians, along with the loves and responsibilities in your life. This is why Jesus pointed out that we are "in" the world but not "of" the world (John 17:13–18). The "in" levels are brought under the authority of the "of" levels, and we know which one needs to take precedence whenever the two levels compete. Hopefully the following chart will assist you in visualizing both the tension and resolution that occur as we learn to distinguish the "of" and "in" layers of passion and of mission under God's direction.

"Of" God-Oriented	Passion "of" Life	Mission "of" Life
Identity and nature	Person of God	Glory of God
"In" World-related	Passions "in" Life	Missions "in" Life
Function and impact	Other loves	Daily responsibilities

In another sense, we cannot imitate the Incarnation. God-Jesus is unique, and so was His incarnation in nature and mission. Very often, Christians equate the practice of Jesus as a pattern for our living. Not without biblical warrant (cf. 1 John 2:6). "What Would Jesus Do?" became a popular slogan among Christians the world over in the late 1990s. "WWJD" bracelets, stickers, necklaces, and T-shirts promoted the imitation of Jesus in life. I was even asked if thought Jesus would wear a WWJD bracelet!

In terms of our subject here, the argument for living a Jesus did goes this way. Jesus knew His mission, so we, too must know our own mission. Jesus evaluated His option and opportunities by His mission; we also must evaluate our options by our mission. Now both statements are true in *themselves*. Only they are not properly understood if we join them wrongly.[2] The crucial issue isn't to merely have a mission for life, but to pursue the *right* mission.

Even non-Christians use the Jesus-paradigm in a superficial way. They study the life of Jesus and notice He had a mission. Consequently, they deduce that they too would be wise to have a mission—a state-able mission. True, the very process of identifying and stating a mission is good for human existence. A life mission certainly helps daily waking and working. So people construct *their* own mission and do *their* own thing—morally neutral missions that enable them to perform better in life. But they could have used Alexander or Napoleon or Churchill instead of Jesus for their mission justification. Some of them do. Anyone can defend any mission as valid using as their justification the fact that Jesus Himself pursued a mission. But in so doing, they miss the very point of Jesus' mission.

As you know, most leaders, good and bad, are mission directed. But Jesus is more than a leader. Yes, Christ share presently recognizable components of effective leadership with other leaders in history. But He is also the Sovereign God and Savior.

Be sure to figure out where you are to be like Jesus and where you are not. You are welcome to mimic His mission as yours, but He is not simply setting a pattern to justify the need of a personal mission or any personal mission. He invites you to work His personal mission into yours. In the third book of this series on a theology of spiritual experience, we will work Jesus' mission in life into our life-purpose. But the mission of Jesus' life is the same as our mission: bringing glory to the Father. "I have brought you glory on earth by completing the work you gave me to do" (John 17:4). This most powerful verse distinguishes the consuming mission *of* Jesus—bringing glory to the Father, by His work in life—His mission *in* life.

Jesus was clear about how this mission applied *in* His life. Early in life He asked His parents, "Why were you searching for me?...Didn't you know I had to be in my Father's house?" (Luke 2:49). Older versions translate Jesus' statement, "I had to be about my Father's business." His parents should have caught on to His mission. In fact, we can read many declarations of the Lord about His mission in life: "My food," said Jesus, "is to do the will of him who sent me and to finish his work" (John 4:34). Or, "I have come down from heaven not to do my will but to do the will of him who sent me" (John 6:38). He distinguished His personal mission from John the Baptist's mission in life, having to finish certain works that were unique to Him: "I have testimony weightier than that of John. For the very work that the Father has given me to finish, and which I am doing, testifies that the Father has sent me (John 5:36). To those following Him, He said, "As long as it is day, we must do the work of him who sent me. Night is coming, when no one can work" (John 9:4).

In John 12, Jesus predicted His own death. Even though He knew that His mission would be excruciatingly difficult, He exposed the disciples to His inner conflict. "Now my heart is troubled, and what shall I say? 'Father, save me from this hour'? No, it was for this very reason I came to this hour" (v. 27). He knew that His mission in human salvation was the means for the Father to glorify His name (v. 28). Jesus came to die on the cross—His mission in life. But through this mission *in* life He brought glory to the Father— the mission *of* His life. John 13:31 repeats Jesus' mission to bring salvation to humanity as the means of bringing glory to the Father. Jesus confidently closed His horrific experience with a triumphant death-cry, "It is finished"(John 19:30). The work didn't finish Him. He finished the work.[3]

As far as we know, neither Jesus nor Paul talked about their own spousal responsibilities. Further, their vocation and ministry merged—what an advantage for those in full-time ministry responsibilities to simplify life. Of course, there are built-in disadvantages in vocational Christian work as well. For instance, we can confuse our sacred mission for spiritual passion, the work itself as love for God, even though the work must proceed from love. John 21:15–17 delineates the sequence—unless you love Jesus you can't shepherd His sheep. Shepherding His sheep is not the same as loving Jesus. I would rather keep ministry and vocation distinct than suffer the consequences of mistaking ministry commitment for spiritual passion.

The connection between the mission *of* life and many missions in life lies in a vital spiritual life.[4] Jesus demonstrates the spiritual connection in His unique way. There was perfect coalescence between His work and God's glory. Jesus was so in touch with His Father that His works could be ruly seen as His Father's work, and His Father's work as His work (cf. John 14:10). His words are the same as His Father's. "For I did not speak of my own accord, but the Father who sent me commanded me what to say and how to say it" (John 12:49). "I tell you the truth, the Son can do nothing by himself; he can do only what he sees his Father doing, because whatever the Father does the Son also does" (John 5:19).

We can't do what Jesus did in His unique Sonship with the Father, but He demonstrates that the way to find coalescence between our mission to make God look great and our missions in life, is to bring them under God's will and weight. That means I must live deeply in touch with the norms, expectations, and desires of the persons of the Trinity in every aspect of life.

Also, the segments of Jesus' life are different than mine. He didn't have a wife or kids. Therefore, He sectored His life differently. His purpose in life was unique, as are yours and mine. He was uniquely qualified for His mission in life. He set His face like a flint to die on a cross and bring salvation to the world (Luke 9:51). While we are beneficiaries of Jesus' mission in life, our missions in life are unique. We vector life differently than He did. Yet we share with Him the ulterior mission of life—to make God look great!

Our salvation foundation unites the "of" and "in" levels of Passion and passions, Mission and missions. Our *spirituality*—foundation maintenance—centers, connects, coordinates, and connects both levels. Again, when the "of" and "in" levels polarize or create conflict, always choose the "of" level. The priority of the "of" level over the "in" level finds clarification in the Godward versus civilian responsibilities. While one must render allegiance to God and Caesar accordingly (Luke 20:25), "we must obey God rather than men" (Acts 5:29).[5]

A "grand theory of everything" must include everything to be grand. If God's glory is the great, grand, governing core of an Intentional Life, we must bring every aspect of human life under its effects.[6] All aspects of life must be within its scope. Each aspect of life must be under its rule. We could be founded, wise, and passionate for God, and still build a random life, intentionally or unintentionally. We may even leave an unfinished building. So how could we go about building an intentional first floor? And beyond?

I suggest that you segment life in order to govern, integrate, and furnish it well.

SEGMENTING DIMENSIONS

Managua, the capital city of Nicaragua, is a nightmare for tourists looking for street addresses. The city also tests mailmen, policemen, and firemen. Streets don't have names and houses lack numbers. As a small town made up of people who sustained relationships without these vital conveniences, there was little problem in locating its residents. But an earthquake that devastated the city in 1972 moved people to the outskirts. Streets "sprang up randomly, with virtually no zoning or supervision." People began to state their addresses in relation to real or imaginary local landmarks. Visitors were given the following directions: "From where the gate of El Retiro Hospital used to be, two blocks toward the lake, one block down." Fire crews, and police cars were often delayed because of difficulties in figuring out addresses. The only advantage of the confusion was that the taxmen were late too!

Does the Managua situation sound like your life? Has random growth led to a chaotic sprawl? Has your life sprung up so rapidly and haphazardly that you are lost? Well, the

Nicaraguan Post Office remedied the problem by dividing the city into quadrants, giving each street, house, and business a number of its own.[7] That's what we will do with your random life. We'll segment your life so someone (including you) can make sense of it. Your immediate response may be that of Managua's residents upon hearing the plan. "This is too complicated," they complained. "We are comfortable with our old ways!" However, if you desperately need help, you'll be thankful for a new pattern of life. In terms of your complicated, random life, you can begin finding mission, direction, even order.

I invite you to consider distributing life—"the human thing"—into three major segments. Most of us experience three areas of living:

Personal Life

Family Life

Work Life[8]

These areas reflect major life responsibilities. Of course these are not hard divisions or compartments, but simply a convenient distribution of life for personal understanding of daily and repeated experience. They connect deeply around the person who is living the personal life. It is "my" life, but it is my life in relationship to my self, family, and work. The personal segment deeply affects the others.

Repetition is a critical feature of these areas—the reason I call it "missions in life." Repetition in kind (I do the same kinds of things) and time (each day I wake up around the same time and go to bed about the same time) represent general characteristics of particular segments. Missions in life deal with the matters at hand, those to which I must attend repeatedly.

Relationships also form a significant part of every per son's life—our relationship to God, spouse, family, col leagues, etc. Even in the "private" pursuit of excellence othe people are involved.

Built on a passionate love for God, the mission *of* life is t make God look great. These three segments form missior critical paths in applying God's weight to our lives. The mis sion of life is to be accomplished in these missions *in* life– making God look good in its various aspects. Non-Christiar and disobedient Christians do not process or benefit from th positive distinction. By chance or choice, they elevate som angle of life as the mission of life. Their confusion normall derives from whatever demands the most time. A man ma shape his mission from his vocation. A mother makes her pr school children her mission. Those "missions" are too sma and seasonal for someone who wants to live intentionally. Isn this why, when a busy man loses his job by firing, lay-off, c retirement, he heads off into depression? Or when the childre grow up and out of the house, the middle-aged couple doesn know how to relate to each other? The biblically grand theor of everything comprises time-taking tasks, but the tasks an responsibilities are not the mission of life. The mission of li is to bring the weight of God to bear on all aspects of lif God's glory becomes the ulterior purpose for living.

I find that the call to excellence arises from this hostir of divine glory in one's life. The reason you ought to be th best in your personal, family, and work life is simply becaus you receive, reflect, and refract God's glory on the earth God's weight drives your responsibilities in these segments.

Below I have outlined some helpful categories (only lin ited by time, space, and range of experience) to use in ve toring your life into segments and subsegments toward th

1. PERSONAL LIFE

Spiritual Life

Nurtured by the spiritual disciplines *(see Book One in this series under "passion")*:

Attachment
Love and praise of God

Detachment
Sensitivity to sin
Confession of sin
Spiritual warfare against the world, flesh, and Satan

Alignment
Understanding of and obedience to God's Word
Living a God-ordered, Christ-centered, and Spirit-filled life
Affirming personal identity in relationship to Jesus
Pursuing wisdom
Developing eternal perspectives
Renewing the mind
Discerning God's will
Sensitivity to needs

Engagement
Activities and Service in Mission (see Book Three in this series, under "ministry-life")
Increasing compassion for neighbor
Loved ones
Lost ones—unbelievers and backslidden believers
Lonely ones, strangers, foreigners
Discovering talents
Developing gifts
Meeting opportunities at church, community, the world, etc.

Suffering
General suffering—physical, emotional, and other
Particular suffering—for the sake of Christ

Physical Life

Health
Consumption: food, drink, sex, addictions
Maintenance: sleep, exercise
Other habits: beneficial, detrimental

Intellectual Life

Formal education
Continuing education
Informal education

Financial Life

A view of money
Faithfulness in giving
Stewardship of financial resources in spending, saving, investing

Material Life

Physical dwelling
Appearance: clothes, cosmetics, jewelry, etc.
Transportation

Recreational Life

Leisure, vacation, television, use of free time, etc.

Social Life

Inner, middle, and outer circles of friendship

Other

For example: cultural life, civilian life, professional life *(see below under "Work")*

2. FAMILY LIFE

Spouse
Unconditional love, intimacy,
conflict resolution

Kids
Raising, loving, mentoring,
disciplining, launching

Parents and siblings
Care and love

Extended family
Care and concern

3. WORK LIFE

Occupation
At home, business, institution, or
profession

Work-related issues
People, performance, personal
development, etc.

mission. If you are to bring glory to the Father as your mission, these are areas of your life where God must increase His weight in order for you to reflect His reputation. Your missions in life will then fulfill the mission of life.

I place "work life" in a separate category rather than listing it under "personal life" for two reasons. One, work occupies large portions of our time and energy, providing subsistence existentially, if not monetarily. Two, because of this time and energy consumption, many people tend to mistakenly make their work their life mission. Instead, I ask you to view work as merely a dimension or sector, although an important one, of life.

You may use the list above (and Christians are good at lists!) to identify prayer items for spiritual attention. Here's a revolutionary addition to my prayer-endings that has transformed perspective and invited God's intervention. It keeps with the theme of this chapter. I not only end my prayers "in Jesus' name," but also add, "for the sake of His reputation." I ask God to do whatever enhances His name.

FROM OUTLINING TO VECTORING

As you examine the three segments and subcategories in each of the sectors, I would like you again to ask the following exploratory questions at our three levels of application—What? So what? Now what?

What? What does the Bible say about the issue? We are not addressing preferences and prejudices here. We must find out the precepts of Scripture on each of these issues. Precepts are the clear statements of Scripture that rule a particular area of life. Recently, an acquaintance declared that he is a lone man living with two other people (his wife and daughter). He went on to make a case that his commitment to Jesus in his work brought a sword between him and his family. He believed that contemporary Christianity had made idols of spouses and families. How this man's view can be squared with the commands to love one's family unconditionally depends on the "what" of Scripture, an issue earlier dealt with under the "passion" subject. Some potential conflicts between precepts must be settled when interpreting Scripture with a view to application. In many countries, the foremost business-related question deals with corruption and rampant bribery. What does the Bible say about the matter? You are mature enough to study these subjects. Go ahead and put questions that arise about each of life's segments and sub-segments to the Bible. Do it at your pace. Compile the answers you discern as God's Word comments on particular and pertinent subjects that need your attention.

So What? What does the Bible ask or claim from me regarding each of these areas? The claims of the Bible should be drawn first from the plain precepts of Scripture. However, if you don't see a clear precept in Scripture on a given issue, look for patterns that occur throughout the Bible. The nature

of Scripture is to govern areas of life by means of precep
first, and then pattern. Ask, "What Scriptural pattern must
follow or obey in a given situation? In the light of that pat
tern where should I change?" Patterns are drawn from pre
cepts, practices, and other biblical material. We can draw
prescriptions from Scripture—precept and/or pattern—
because God has given us everything necessary for life and
godliness; because all Scripture is inspired and therefore con
sistent; and because all Scripture is profitable for life. Even
biblical issues that seem, at first glance, to be quite distant
from us turn out to have powerful contemporary application
For example, the instances of "eating meat offered to idols"
or "caring for an alien in the land" fall within the larger pat
tern of "loving your neighbor." Consequently, if God need
to increase His weight in my caring for people of other races
I submit to this prescriptive pattern. We are under the
authority of these biblical patterns. Both precepts and pat
terns are prescriptive.

Now What? How, practically, should I put the Bible into
obedience? How do I go about practicing what the Scripture
teaches (the precept or pattern) and claims (the prescription)
We need the wisdom of mentors and pastors to furnish us
strategies for obedience. Practical strategies are not prescrip
tions—like Scriptural precepts or patterns. Rather, they are
preferences for a particular person or context. I cannot make
these preferences absolute or I would fall into legalism. For
example, one of my two strategic burdens I carry in ministry
is to strengthen the pastoral leaders of weaker economies
This strategy was born out of a variety of factors. I believe
this is the most critical ministry strategy for the health of the
church throughout the world. We can find precepts and pat
terns in the Bible to defend the preference. However, I can't

obligate all Christians or ministries to this particular strategy of obeying the Great Commission by precept or pattern. I can obligate Christians to obey the Great Commission, but not to *this* way of obedience. Where we find other organizations that share similar priorities, we can partner together in *this* way of fulfilling the Great Commission.

Here are three more personal examination questions you can use to immediately apply your heart to wisdom in daily life.

1. In which areas of my life today is God a mere "lightweight"?

Evaluate this according to biblical precepts and come away with three or four areas to which you must give immediate attention. For instance, the Bible exhorts us to not "give up meeting together" (Heb. 10:25). I met a family while speaking at a Family Camp who neglected the church habit because they owned a seven-day-a-week restaurant. Instead, they listened to television evangelists, especially the miracle-working kind, for spiritual intake, and were severely undernourished. While they drank in the ministry of those five days, they were lacking in close relationships with other believers. Their children were devoid of social skills. Worse yet, this family had nowhere to turn in times of joy or need. Clearly, local church involvement was one of their primary dimensions needing immediate attention. God was presently a lightweight in their family in terms of local church involvement—a key component of the personal sector.

2. Where and how can God increase His weight, influence, and presence?

How can God be made to look great in your life? The family running a seven-day-a-week business model considered putting the biblical precept of Christian community into practice. As we discussed the flow of their typical week, they noted that Sunday night was the least busy night at their restaurant. I suggested that they find a church that meets Sunday evenings. Closing the restaurant one evening in order to make time for worship, fellowship, prayer, and teaching would far surpass the benefits of their meager takings. I assured them they would also see the Lord lead them into firmer relational commitments and even timely provision.

Perhaps you experience ongoing conflict with your wife. I remember our eighteenth year of marriage. It didn't seem like Bonnie and I could agree on anything pertaining to life. We held divergent and opposite opinions on everything. Accented by the moral default of a friend of high stature, my trusting wife became afraid of my itinerant lifestyle. On one occasion I remember telling her I would admit I was wrong if she admitted I was right. She asked me to go first! I said, "I'm wrong."

She replied, "You're right!"

But the Scriptures plainly teach that I must care for my wife sacrificially and love her unconditionally. Fortunately, we were committed to each other, our marriage, and to making God look good in our lives. How did we go about increasing His presence in our marriage? As God extended His influence in her life, she found out that she had been wrong all along? No. Don't you believe that statement for a moment, or I will be in deep trouble. That season of conflict is over—at least for the discernible present. We prayed together regularly about our problem. We attended a marriage seminar to focus on our past, to ask and give forgiveness to each other. She graciously doesn't even bring up issues that would reduce my internal image to dust. As God augmented His presence in our personal and marriage life, we found out that we had more energy for the Lord and each other. Our willingness to give God weight in our life—the sacred covenant of marriage—allowed us to go past those days to deeper friendship and intimacy.

3. What areas of my life need spiritual attention and action?

Now that you have identified some areas of your life that need God's increasing weight, prioritize three areas and write out date-stamped action steps that will begin to make God look good in these segments of your life.

I am presently struggling in financial stewardship areas between risk tolerance and keeping up with inflation. Since my risk tolerance is very, very low, I have kept monies in a low-interest-paying, insured bank. Over the last few years, friends have prevailed in convincing me that investing funds in the stock market is relatively safe and provides a higher return on investment. The turning point occurred when someone pointed out to me an elemental fact of economics: "After taxes and inflation, you are actually losing money in those low interest accounts." Of course, I know some who have lost nearly everything attempting to assuage greed with highly leveraged portfolios. Recent wild, market swings have made a lot of chickens out of bulls and bears.

Having consulted with others whose risk tolerance is at my level, I have made appropriate investing a priority focus in life for the next three months. I am moving a part of our savings into an asset management account with the kind of long-term view that makes allowances for the swings in the market. My date-stamped action step calls for a December 31 deadline. I'll make September 1 of each year the cut-off date to consider moving deadwood accounts to better paying investments. If you have another opinion on this matter, you are welcome to contact me!

All of us need to consider our stewardship values more often. I admit I don't have the time or the inclination to read the back pages of newspapers, let alone the quarterly reports of money managers. However, appropriate stewardship brings God more glory. I have failed. I confess. I'm learning. I will act. I can always change the frequency of my attention to financial matters as circumstances change and needs arise. But I will neither neglect these issues nor allow them to consume me.

This short chapter has covered vast territory. We have vectored life, setting it about its missions under the ulterior mission of making God look great in each segment that needs spiritual attention. Until you begin to discern your segments and track your present condition, you will not move forward. So use pen, stylus, or keyboard to evaluate how God is doing in the key segments of your life. Ask God how He can look better and increase His weight where He is not receiving your appropriate response and recognition. You will be amazed at His Spirit's conviction and proposals for your intentional consideration in application. Write them down and plan a course of obedience. This basic process will move you well on the way and at your own pace toward more intentional living.

Integrating Life

I n a speech to the graduates of Lafayette College, historian Doris Kearns Goodwin recalled her fascinating glimpse into the mindset of former U.S. president Lyndon B. Johnson:

> On the surface, [President Johnson] should have had everything in the world to be grateful for in those last years. His career in politics had reached its peak in becoming the President of the United States. He had all the money he needed to pursue any leisure activity he wanted. He owned a spacious ranch in the country, a penthouse apartment in the city, a half dozen cars equipped with traveling bars, a sailboat, a speedboat, a movie theater in his own home, and this amazing swimming pool that was

The life that hath not
willed itself to be,
Must clasp the life that
willed, and be at peace;
Or, like a leaf wind-blown,
through chaos fell;
A life-husk into which the
demons go,
And work their will, and
drive it to and fro;
A thing that neither is, nor
yet can cease,
Which uncreation can
alone release.

GEORGE MACDONALD

equipped with floating rafts, on top of which were floating desks and floating notepads and floating sandwiches, so that you could work at every moment.

Then she ended her remarks in this way:

A month before he died, he spoke to me with immense sadness in his voice. He said he was watching the American people absorbed in a new president, forgetting him, forgetting, he feared, even the great civil rights laws that he had passed, and was beginning to think that his quest for immortality had been in vain. Perhaps, he said, he would have been better off focusing more time and attention on his family.[1]

Lyndon Johnson seems to have acknowledged the segments of family and work, but succumbed to nonstop confusion of those segments that resulted in eventual regret. Granted, a short-term imbalance that jumbles priorities during seasonal spurts of hectic activity marks the life of any leader. But an anticipated and managed busyness with the consent of the key stakeholders of your life—God, spouse, family—can be part of a life acceptable to God. However, sustained confusion of the segments inevitably degenerates into the "life-husk into which the demons go," as George MacDonald so aptly put it. So what then may we do to avoid final regretful sentiments? They can be prevented by vectoring and integrating the segments of life for long-term balance and continued obedience.

POLICY MAKING

The next two chapters are going to require prayer, thought, and written reflection. I suggest you implement this integration strategy with prayerful reflection at any time your balance becomes skewed or when the demons of anxiety arise and you feel like quitting. Perhaps you can use changing seasons—New Year's Day, birthdays (especially big ones!), and vacations to refresh life-policies towards personal mission.

To integrate our mission into life, first we will rank life-segments in terms of importance. Ranking them is not a one-time event (though the first time will require the most discipline), and it will necessitate special attention each time you change seasons in life. However, the consistent ranking is always *personal, family,* and *work* segments, in that order. Do not rearrange this hierarchy, especially the latter two. (A friend tearfully confessed that he finally cut down from a 110-hour work week to a more modest 75-hour work week! His wife filed for divorce last month.) Then we make and live out the policies to integrate the segments.

Part of integrating life evokes and reaffirms neglected segments. One of the benefits that flow from segmenting life—we have to face all the areas we have claimed are important to us but which we haven't been treating as important by the way we actually live—is to *recover lost priorities.* Here we realize what we must shore-up and defend them at all costs, before going on to new territory that we must pursue and capture.

Having prioritized these segments and ranked them, you then will write out "policies" for those three areas of life.[2] These personalized policies address your wishes, wants, and mandates for each segment, which will be addressed in the section below under "strategies." As you work through these exercises, keep in mind the importance of interacting with Scripture on how you intend to glorify God in the large areas of everyday life—personal life, family life, and work life.

Imagine the Holy Trinity as your Governing Board, with the Lord Jesus as the President. In this scenario, Scripture provides for the policy-making in your life, and you serve as the Executive Vice President to personalize and implement it. Get this line of authority straight.

Policies reveal values—the implications of our passion for God. They will also show our perspectives, our biblical bias, as they dictate the functioning of the three segments. The Board and the President have established your mission, but you, the Executive Vice President, remain responsible for strategies, tactics, procedures, and action. You will report to the President and the Board, who define your mission, establish policy, and provide empowering authority.

Here are some broad, personalized policy statements I have written to express how I want to love God enough (passion) to make Him look good (mission):

- ➤ *Personal life*—A joyful, dependent, growing walk with God, His people, and creation by regularly evaluating, correcting, planning, and implementing God's will in all discernible areas of my life.

- ➤ *Family life*—A loving husband, father, son, brother, and friend in leading my family to spiritual and personal maturity.

- ➤ *Work life*—Promote Jesus Christ in the world as I give my best to multiple vocational roles and ministry gifts.

Write out your own personalized policy statement for each of the three large areas of life. Do not work with the subsegments yet. Within these broad policies that Scripture addresses, you possess immense freedom to express desires, make decisions, pursue resources, seize opportunities, and mplement choices. Ask the Lord to help you gather the breadth and depth of life under their umbrella.

As you mature in the spiritual governance process, you will write out policies at the sublevels in sequence—personal levels, family levels, and work levels. Policies at sublevels are the means to the ends. Large-level policies are the missions you pursue in life. You evaluate all you do at the narrower levels in correspondence with larger-level policies.

STRATEGIES

From life-policy, you go on to life-strategies in integrating life. You must attend to your mission—the mission of glorifying God in the various missions in life. I asked you to divide life into three larger segments. I now ask you to make a wide-ranging "wish list" and then pare it down to reflect key life-strategies. I challenge you to spend twenty-four hours with nothing but your Bible, pen and notebook, or computer to record your personal response to soul-mission in vectoring and integrating life's strategic priorities. You will be preparing three intense lists.

"Wish" List

You can create this list for the sake of dreaming. The adolescent who dreams night (and day) about a television star, who wishes he would win the lottery, or vividly imagines himself driving a new McLaren F1 is "wishing." My wish to play the piano is just that! Amuse yourself with this blue-sky, unrealistic process. Write down everything that appeals to you, all your wishes, what you covet, your cravings—worthy and worthless, sinful and neutral, wholesome and stupid. Only don't let anyone find the list!

You want to keep this wish list private because it will

often reveal the darkness of your soul, the shallowness o
your life. You might find hints of depth, but little else. As vis
ceral creatures, we tend to let our senses define the good
true, and beautiful in the most relative terms. You can also
evaluate your sensitivity to the Lord by looking at the list
You may want to fall on your knees and repent at your tri
fling with silliness, superficiality, and sin. The more mature
you are, the less moronic your list will be. But write the lis
out for fun and insight. If you're honest, you'll be surprised
by your shallowness. (No, you are not going to see mine. I've
already shredded it.)

Wishes reveal our conceptions and misconceptions o
perfection. Usually these perfections are reserved for heaven
Certain religious views of heaven, e.g., multiple wives on
demand, represent little more than their wish list. We'll leave
those wish lists to the religions to fulfill. One invests little
more than emotional energy into a wish list.

On the wish list you can write down anything you desire
but since you are neither omnipotent nor omniscient, this wil
be mostly an exercise in wishful thinking. After this fun list
ing, you will want to work on priorities that keep with your
policies so you can turn them into strategies. Eventually, you
will have to strategize by defining priorities, setting bound
aries, and utilizing assets in the ongoing demands of life.

"Want" List

We need to go beyond a wish list to a want list.[3] A want list
is your view of a fulfilled, complete life. Again, write these
"wants" under your three life segments. My want list accord
ing to the segments contains the following desires:

Personal:

Spiritual—a sense of God's pleasure in everything I do

Intellectual—critically keep up with contemporary world news, trends, philosophies

Financial—make giving to the Lord's work my number one expense

Physical—ongoing physical exercise program, etc.

Family:

Bonnie—to be best of friends

Kids—get them the finest and highest possible education

Parents—visit once a week, call several times a week

Mother-in-law—bring once a year to visit

Siblings—extensive regular contact, once a month at least, and reunion every two years

Work:

Writing—publish one book per year

Speaking—proclaiming Christ in every country of the world

A want list is a fine tool to help you not only get in touch with your drives, but also help you later to align your priorities with your policies. If priorities and policies don't correspond, you'll experience imbalance. If motivations, priorities, and policies do not harmonize, you'll feel dissonance. But we want more than internal consonance; we also want external balance. Therefore, I would like you now to create a "without" list from your want list.

"Without" List

You can write out your wants but usually not all of them are what you *really* want. You need to write out a *sine qua non* list (Latin, "that without which")—a "necessities of life" list. This is a list composed of that which you cannot live "without" in those three personal segments, and perhaps their subsegments.

How do we write a without list? How can we scratch out or scale down expectations into a *sine qua non* list? How do we rid our life of greeds and work on the needs? Here we rely on the leadership of God's Holy Spirit and His Word. The Bible and the Holy Spirit work in tandem like the needle of a compass and the presence of a guide in an unknown, dark place. We will study their roles in future guidance later. For now, it is important to affirm that the Bible addresses life at all levels, including sublevels.

Some biblical life policies give you a range of applicational choices because they provide wide interpretive scope. For instance, financially contributing to God's work provides a broad applicational range—we can give cheerfully, regularly, proportionately. To increase or decrease giving according to income is a spiritual principle—as long as we do it joyfully and regularly. It is a spacious policy guiding your giving to God. Yet other biblical guidance policies are stated clearly and definitively so we are to be governed by them. "You shall not commit adultery" mandates faithfulness to one's spouse. Not up for interpretation.

Coming up with a without list is difficult emotionally but easier than you think. Using your want list, follow these steps to determine your without list.

1. Delete sinful wants.

Some of your wants are plainly sinful and you need to get rid of them immediately. You may want a different spouse from the one you've got, but the number of spouses we are allowed is very narrow—one. There is no point in writing another spouse on your "want" list. Such an "item" may be found in your unwritten wish list, but wish lists are for the immature anyway. As much as you would like a different set of kids, you can't easily replace them. Beware! They may be writing your name on their "discard" lists too. You certainly can't bring God glory by pursuing sinful wants.

2. Pray over your want list.

Ask the Lord to show you your weaknesses for inappropriate wants, although they may be neutral. Be sensitive to His leadership, to His prompts in Scripture, and to your conscience. I recall a time I was looking at changing cars. I knew we needed a bigger car to accommodate growing kids. Should we move into the bottom end of the luxury market, even if we could afford it? As I eyed a fancy car driving past me, my eyes fell in my devotional book to the psalmist's prayer, "Keep my eyes off worthless things." I chuckled over the timely direction. Actually, that car was on a wish list, not a want list, and shouldn't be on my without list.

Remove anything on your want list about which you sense spiritual doubt. Leave anything that you can pray about wholeheartedly. As you pray about those specific items, you will sense an increasing conviction about leaving other certain items out. If you don't leave these out, you will be operating from presumption rather than faith. Be radically obedient at this very meaningful time. Wield an editor's sharp pen in scratching that line off your without list.

You will also need to take practical considerations into account. Sensible doubt regularly accompanies practical decisions: Would I put up with the color of that expensive car? Can I afford the auto insurance? Do I need that much space? Some friends of mine in the Philippines did not drive an expensive vehicle because that was a giveaway to would-be "carjackers" that they were wealthy. A practical consideration, to drive a Toyota and not a Mercedes even though they could afford the latter in their want list, pointed to wisdom.

3. Set boundaries around yourself.

Look for prudent boundaries provided by the implications of scriptural principles at the level of each of your wants. "Don't go into debt" translates into paying cash for anything that depreciates in value. Back to cars as an illustration of the contemporary psyche. Even if that new vehicle looks enticing, your ruthless adherence to not go into debt will clear it off your without list. Let it remain on your want list, but get it off your without list.

When Lexus automobiles were new and the rage of our materialistic-minded city, I experienced an unexpected offer. After speaking to a group of rather wealthy young entrepreneurs, I was riding down the elevator of the University Club in Dallas. One man, obviously stirred by the talk, took out his key ring, removed the key to his Lexus, and gave it to me with the words, "I hope I make it into the kingdom." In order not to embarrass him (and to let him muse over his impulsive response), I accepted the key. We got off the elevator and talked. I told him that I had set some boundaries around my possessions. As the head of a nonprofit corporation that was supported by donors, I couldn't drive something like that expensive road beauty. I didn't want to have to mumble explanations or make excuses for anything to anybody. More importantly, I told him as I handed back his key, I was interested in his comment about "making it into the kingdom." I met with him later to secure his sole trust in the Lord Christ.

When I told the story of his offer to my kids, they could hardly believe their dad had actually turned down a free Lexus. But wise boundaries which attend my ministry kept me from putting a Lexus on my without list. I don't think it was even on my wish list. Automobile insurance alone, with three teenagers, was a practical consideration. Further, he didn't offer the car again after we secured his inclusion in the kingdom!

4. Prioritize among competing "neutral" wants.

When priorities compete, you've got to simplify your life. Priorities and wants of "don't go into debt" and "drive a luxury car" may compete. You have to choose one over the other as you write out your *sine qua non* list. Eventually, you want only *noncompeting priorities* on your without list.

In prioritizing, you also need to be sensitive to the seasons of your life. "Season appropriateness" will help you with your without list. At the moment, my children are into the pre-human stage, euphemistically called "teenager." While I desire to proclaim Christ in every country of the world (see above) as a life want, it is not an immediate "without" because I need to carve out time to be with my growing kids. They represent a big part of my world in this season of life. We hardly see each other during weekdays, so I've got to work it out to be home on weekends. The tension is real: How can I keep my overseas schedule (a want) and stay home more? For now, my without list dictates that I limit the number of my domestic weekend-long engagements, while keeping up the overseas forays. Once the kids leave home (and I think they will), I can be gone a bit more. Perhaps my wife will travel at least three times a year with me (another want), but this feature is not on my without list at the moment.

What you "want" in one season of your life will not necessarily be a desire or interest in another. It could become a "without" or a "wish" in another season. In my early twenties, I really thought I wouldn't be able to live "without" becoming a musician. But the musical goals gradually became a "want" as my seasons changed and as new gifts and opportunities emerged. Now music shares, with other previous desires, a "has been" category on a distant wish list. I find young people "wanting" to start off at an economic level where their parents ended their careers. That "want" could be unrealistic and should certainly not be on their "without" list, simply because and normally speaking, it is not yet the right season of their lives.

Kevin McCarthy, in his book *The On-Purpose Person: Making Your Life Make Sense,* suggests writing out your wants for each segment of your life on a sheet of paper, alternating between writing them at the top and bottom of that sheet, and then playing a tournament. Like a draw sheet or bracket in a tournament, match wants against each other, only advance the wants you really want, to the next round. Those that make it to the right side of the paper are your most meaningful wants, demanding your highest attention. You don't eliminate the other wants, they are just lower priorities.[4] You will then come up with a list of core wants in the major segments of life. I would add that your final list should be made up of *non*-competing priorities. Also, you don't need a single priority in these three segments of personal, family, and work life. You may come up with more than one, but be sure they don't compete *equally* for spirit, vision, time, money, and energy.

Of course, you don't play the tournament rounds by making "instinctual" choices, or even just by "thinking it through," as McCarthy suggests.[5] You play them by reflecting and receiving the policies that Scripture lays down for your life. If you have decided to pay for your kids' college, but a beautiful home presents an opportunity to buy and get into unmanageable debt, you better choose the former, because of the scriptural priority of people over things.

"Everything is permissible for me—but not everything is beneficial," says Paul (1 Cor. 6:12). You have to gauge your heart and internal dissonance while waiting on God for clearance. And what is permissible to some may prove unacceptable for you (1 Cor. 10:23). I don't mind that friends or even Christian leaders drive high-priced cars. I don't even mind that they often drive me around in them! But I know that owning such a vehicle would not benefit the ministry I represent in view of unwritten expectations of those who give sacrificially for economically poor beneficiaries worldwide.

Again take that Scriptural priority of people over things: "Nobody should seek his own good, but the good of others" (1 Cor. 10:24). God really doesn't have problems with your driving luxury cars unless your motives are wrong. Why do you want another car? For enjoyable transportation? For transportation and personal validation? If you want a new car at the material level, but that conflicts with your providing adequately for your kids, you will have to drive an older car. If you can't live without the latter, come to terms with your selfish and idolatrous penchants. Evaluate through the lens of Scripture where your real identity is found. And wait till your internal convictions are clear by immersing yourself in Scripture, so you can "grow in the grace and knowledge of our Lord and Savior Jesus Christ" (2 Peter 3:18). The exercise will seem tedious and complicated unless you craft good policy ahead of time. Every decision calls for a thorough baptism in the Scripture at the levels of knowledge, will, and obedience.

5. *Scale down expectations or the means to those expectations.*

Living as we do in the abundance of the West, we face a significant challenge trying to develop a sense of proportion about our wants and needs. The Buddhist analysis of the egotistical problem of "desire" contains some merit. It agrees with the biblical view that the Self, in its craving and lusts, causes unnecessary frustration. We tell Buddhists, however, that we can't fully give up desires, for that pursuit of giving up desires is actually a desire in itself. I received a humorous birthday card depicting the Dalai Lama opening a package, finding it empty, and exclaiming: "Nothing! What I always wanted!" Further, while we are against the egotistical "I," we are not against the psychological "I." "I" am the person who has to deny my Self. Also, it is not desire itself that is the problem, but the source, motivation, time, and quality of the desires. The apostle Paul gave us a delightful description of this interplay between the egotistical and psychological self when he described his spiritual life, "I have been crucified with Christ and I no longer live, but Christ lives in me. The life I live in the body, I live by faith in the Son of God, who loved me and gave himself for me" (Gal. 2:20).

Further, let's reserve some things for heaven. We "want" everything right now. Look at my want list above. That's really my without list, except the one item that reads, "proclaiming Christ in every country of the world." Not only does that "want" compete with my present academic demands and family season, I can "season" it by asking about the motives of my want. Why do I want to preach in every country of the world? Just because it is a wonderful thing to do? Because I want to be among the first to do so? I can also ask questions about the quality of that expectation. Is there a way I could proclaim Christ in every country of the world, other than by personal presence? What about proclamation through books, videos, tapes, or even other people? The latter question seems to be presently taking shape by

God's sovereign provision of opportunities. I suggest that under God you expect nothing but anticipate much. Do not fall into discontentment or unbelief.

Keep these five factors in mind as you construct your *sine qua non* list.

> ### Constructing a "Without" List from a "Want" List
>
> 1. Delete sinful wants.
> 2. Pray over your want list.
> 3. Set boundaries for yourself.
> 4. Prioritize among competing "neutral" wants.
> 5. Scale down expectations or the means to those expectations.

A time-management expert, business legend has it, impressed high-achievers with an unforgettable point. He carefully placed a dozen fist-sized rocks in a wide-mouthed, glass jar and asked, "Is the jar full?"

"Yes," they replied.

"Really?" He poured a pail-full of gravel into the jar. As he shook the container, the gravel found spaces to lodge themselves. "Is the jar full now?" he quizzed them.

Having caught on, they answered, "Probably not."

"Good!" he replied. He brought out a beach bucket of sand and poured a handful into the jar. The sand went into the space left between the rocks and the gravel.

Once more he asked the question, "Is this jar full?"

"No!" the class barked.

Again he said, "Good!" He poured a mug of water to fill the jar to the brim.

He wanted to drive home the point: "What is the lesson in this illustration?"

One immediately blurted the obvious: "No matter how full your schedule is, if you try really hard, you can always fit some more things into it!"

"No," the speaker replied. "That's not the point. The illustration teaches us that if you don't put the big rocks in first, you'll never get them in at all."[6]

This powerful illustration can be used for a number of understandings, to develop three pointers for application. For example, in time-management—the nooks and crannies of minutes should not be neglected so that the hours will not be wasted. In communicating our spiritual life trilogy, I like to refer to them as three big "Life Rocks" that must be put in place or spilled out in order to start up again. Or, to conclude this chapter, the three big rocks refer to your writing out and implementing policy in the three segments of life so as to balance and integrate these sometimes competing segments around the mission of life. Unless you put these life policies for the three segments in place first, it will be very difficult to work back to them. If you write and live them out, your life will clasp the order of making God look great, of grasping the weight of God's glory in your life, instead of being flayed around like "a leaf windblown."

T.A.R.G.E.T.-ing Life

Missions in life deal with what we do regularly and repeatedly—the matters at hand. We can't escape these matters at hand. They kind of hang around us till the end! Matters at hand relate to the three major segments of life—personal, family, and work life. We can go about wishing we vectored and integrated them better or differently, or we can address these intentionally. I borrow a gripping and applicable illustration for managing these segments.

> *Great minds have purposes, others have wishes.*
> — WASHINGTON IRVING

In a military sense, the commander must know that of the three hills that he or she possesses on the right-hand side of the battlefield, the one on the left and the one on the right can be abandoned, but the one in the middle must be defended to the last person because from it is an unobstructed view over half the battlefield.[1]

You've got to defend the major segments of life at all costs, so that you can go further in life's mission. Your life is the middle hill that must be protected so you can accomplish the mission. The "three hills" approach to life's segments can be seized by "self-lovers" and "self-haters" for unbiblical nuances. Using the illustration, narcissism places the Self at the center of the ultimate defense—defending the base, capturing the advantage, and viewing the battlefield. Narcissism wants you to protect yourself at all costs since you are the ultimate one. Buddhists rightly attack that view, as does Jesus in His comments on denying Self.

However, you don't have to apologize to the narcissists or self-negators for aiming your personal priority towards these larger ends. As noted earlier, unlike the Buddhist, we affirm the "one" (the psychological "I") who has to defend the hill. There has to be an "I" strengthened in its underlying passion who overflows into the mission of glorifying God. Honoring God in those three areas defends the nonnegotiable mountain. We defend our lives not as an end, but as a means to the mission. We subscribe to a policy for each of the segments and, as we spiritually mature, for subsegments to make God look good.

As you reflect on and implement the strategies of previous chapters, remember that a conflict between priorities is better than a conflict between policies, but no easier to resolve. Scaling down your wants won't come without an internal fight. But you are attempting to bring God's weight into your life. You will have to work through the hard task of giving yourself (and perhaps others) legitimate scriptural reasons for your new "without" list. You will no longer be living by the rule of "whatever everyone else is doing or pursuing." Revisit the list every few years because life-seasons change, perspectives shift, and best of all, you yourself will change.

Each of us stands at differing levels of maturity and will be dealing with different priorities in terms of ongoing life-missions. In the spiritual life process, as you advance in knowledge, understanding, and commitment, you will find yourself in increasing specific submission to the Trinity in the details of life. The Trinity of God (your Governing Board) has granted you the permission and authority to execute your choices within their policies as found in Scripture. When you break scripturally-based policy, you sin by omission or commission. When confronted, you undertake the discipline of confession to make matters right with God and neighbor—submission. At other times, when you compromise your boundaries or break priorities, you will fall on your knees before God to examine your heart. These are the outcomes of a passion for God in your life mission. Now using the "without" list that you hammered out in the last chapter, let's look at how you can begin to construct a "work" list.

A "WORK" LIST

Your "work" list identifies aspects of your life that you must work on immediately—your mandates. Among these will be areas of neglect that you have identified and confessed for omission or poor stewardship. These will also be aspects of life that demand immediate attention, because your mission is to glorify God in all areas of your life. A work list enables you to put life energies into value-based objectives or task-based goals. I prefer the term "objectives," rather than "goals," for the simple reason that the former (reflecting *knowledge, values, ends, strategies*) includes the latter (reflecting *action, tasks, programs, assignments, aims*), especially in thinking deep and long.

Goals aim toward intermediate targets allowing you to accomplish long-term or short-term objectives or ends. The objectives will substantially remain and sustain you through out your life, while goals are more circumstantially sensitiv and adaptable. Actually only in the ulterior purpose of God glory do all objectives and goals, ends and aims meet. Or, t use mission language, the more clear and passionate you ar about the mission *of* your life (ulterior purpose), the cleare and passionate you can be about the missions in your lif (objectives), and the clearer and passionate you can be abou the goals in your life.

For immediate action we need goals. The "goals" her are not self-motivated, self-generated, self-activated Nev Year resolutions. Rather, spiritual power from divine lov combined with spiritual motivation toward divine glory an guided by the truth of God's Word encourages, enables, an empowers you in setting and reaching goals. Objectives carr a contingent ring to them and reflect action-evokin "wants." Instead, you want want-implementing action— goals for assignments, tasks, and action. Something to whic you can attend to right away. "Unless objectives are con verted into action, they aren't objectives; they are dreams."

To start your work list, first write out a single goal at th level or sublevel on which you want to work. I suggest you us one page for each goal. You can use more paper if needed Maybe your first goal is to start setting them! Goals need to b on T.A.R.G.E.T.

GOALS ON T.A.R.G.E.T

Goals on T.A.R.G.E.T. (an acronym) will exhibit the follow ing features.

Tangible: Tangible goals are ones that you can see an specify in your mind. They are mission-related goals dealin with ongoing issues, with what is necessary for a life tha makes God look good. If you can't see or specify your goals, they are not clear in your head. "Soon I'll do good to a neighbor" is not a tangible goal to my mind. It shows a good heart, but isn't specific enough for action. What kind of good? Which neighbor? How soon is soon?

Adjustable: If you can't *adjust* your goals, you are enslaved to false ideas about your abilities. You actually carry too lofty a view of ability to execute life. If you assume that a task cannot be done unless it is done by you in your way, you have given little room for God's role, help from others, or changing circumstances. Allow for adjustment because life is unpredictable. By the mercy of God, He allows us a measure of order, in spite of our desire to be in control. Yet life throws curves in the most unexpected ways. Many leaders are extremely focused in order not to waste time, but also get frustrated when higher priorities demand greater attention than they thought was necessary. You may not be able to attend to the needs of two neighbors tomorrow, and then a third—of whose critical need you were unaware—may come to your attention. You will need to adjust. However, if you have to adjust or postpone dates of goals frequently, I suggest that you find an accountability system (often a partner?) who will enable you to check on your process and implementation of goals.

Realistic: If you can't *reach* or accomplish your goals, you are into imaginary castle-building, not building a life. "Today I'll write letters of encouragement to two colleagues" is more likely to be accomplished than making a goal to "Go through my database and write to every acquaintance, neighbor, and friend sometime soon."

Generative: Goals carry generative power. Not only do they generate joy and eventually affect self-concepts, they incite action, provide stamina, and focus daily life. Good and right goals generate action. They also stimulate sub-conscious inclinations that attract your attention and unleash your energy. "Doing good to a neighbor" generates obedience, but also instigates ideas as to how a particular neighbor could be helped. Could I pick up his newspaper for him? Could I phone to encourage her once a week? Would I arrange for meals during his time of illness?

Explainable: Clear goals are not only tangible, but also explainable. If you can't communicate your goals, they are not clear in your own head, nor are they clear to those around you. If I can't explain a goal to my family—"I will compare auto insurance rates by April 15"—I have not understood it well myself. You should be able to communicate, justify, and restate your goals. The explainability of a goal allows an accountability system to check its quality and your progress. In the above example of helping a neighbor, I would ask why I chose to send a neighbor money instead of arranging for gifts to be delivered to him. Questions like these allow me to think about the goals that I am putting in place rather than just writing a bunch of good-intentioned statements on a piece of paper. Explainability allows for evaluation and accountability.

Trackable: Trackable goals are *time*-stamped. If you don't time- or date-stamp your goals, your plan will not carry gravity. You will be confused and tired. "By tomorrow evening, I will write a letter of encouragement to my neighbors," allows you to set the time, but also to extend it into late evening if needed. "By tomorrow evening, I'll write notes of encouragement to my neighbors, Mr. Jones and Mrs. Smith," allows me to track the accomplishment of the goals. If you can't *track* your goals, you won't know when you have reached them.[3]

If you are better at goal-making than goal-managing, share our objectives and goals with someone who will keep you accountable. (See place for accountability signature below on worksheet.) This accommodation may not always be needed; it depends on the quality of your goals, your motivation levels, and implementation habits. My suggestion is if you have to "adjust" the date (adjustability is a necessary feature of goals) more than twice, solicit the help of an accountability partner. Depending on the issue, your accountability partner could be a family member or a close friend.

T.A.R.G.E.T. WORKSHEET

A simple planning worksheet helps me (and my kids) on everything from strategizing for homework assignments to long-term mega-projects.[4] The less complicated a worksheet, the more apt you are to use it. I find many leadership books provide complicated grids for personal planning. You have to go through a major (and often expensive) initiation process at times. The simplicity of this chart commends itself to your action. My children used it for school projects before they were teenagers.

On the following page is a blank worksheet which you may copy, or use as a model for a worksheet of your own design.

In the completed sample worksheet on page 129 I illustrate these tracking steps in the context of my financial stewardship, an area I told you I needed to work on. First, I prayed for direction at a time when we needed a little more space at home. With kids growing into extra-long and large, should we remodel or buy a larger home? What can we do "without"? What shouldn't we do "without"? Our home is bigger than most pastoral leaders' homes in Africa, Asia, and Latin

T.A.R.G.E.T. WORKSHEET

OBJECTIVE
Ongoing value-based statements or strategies denoting *ends*

My Objective:

GOAL
Short- or long-term steps or *aims* (Tangible, Adjustable, Realistic, Generative, Explainable, Trackable)

My Goal:

Critical Steps What?	Check-up Dates When?	Person(s) Responsible Who?	Needed Resources How?	End Result or Product
1.				
2.				
3.				

Signature _____ Date _____

Accountability Partner's Signature *(if needed)* _____

T.A.R.G.E.T. WORKSHEET

OBJECTIVE

MAKING GOD LOOK GOOD IN MY FINANCES.

GOAL
(Tangible, Adjustable, Realistic, Generative, Explainable, Trackable)

TO MOVE $____ FROM THE BANK TO A RELIABLE
FUND ACCOUNT BY SEPTEMBER 1.

(For those who seek initiation into this new process, note that the written goal is specific in terms of amount, account, and time, and therefore measurable. I am scheduled to leave for South Africa on August 20 and hope to have this transfer completed by then. The days before I leave are busier than normal. I could move the deadline to December 31 if needed. If my wife and I decide to do some interior redecorating in our home, I may need to adjust the amount to a more realistic goal. The date is time-stamped and definite.)

Critical Steps What?	Check-up Dates When?	Person(s) Responsible Who?	Needed Resources How?	End Result or Product
1. RESEARCH 3 FUNDS	AUGUST 15	RAMESH	MATERIALS/ PROSPECTUS OF FUNDS	CHOICE OF 1 RELIABLE FUND
2. UNIFY BANK ACCTS.	AUGUST 17	RAMESH	CONSULT 2 EXPERIENCED FRIENDS	ALL DATA (PH., FAX, ON-LINE) SET
3. DEPOSIT CHECK TO NEW ACCT.	AUGUST 19	RAMESH	VISIT BANK	1 BANK ACCT. FOR 6-MTH. LIQUIDITY
4. CHECK PERFORMANCE IN DEC.	DEC. 31	RAMESH	SEND CHECK	DEPOSIT APPEARS IN STATEMENT
5. CHANGE FUND IF NEEDED		RAMESH		FUND OUT-PERFORMS BANK

Signature _____ Date _____

Accountability Partner's Signature *(if needed)* _____

America, but less conspicuous than the homes of most "opin-ion" leaders with whom I work in these lands. But size is not the issue. Wisdom is. Our children are now too old to sleep with their parents when we entertain overnight guests. They also seek a measure of privacy. For the last eleven years a three-bedroom home was adequate, and we were content. Should we remodel or move?

Until we make a decision, should I keep the money in a bank account bearing the least interest, or move it to a more risky, higher-interest bearing account? Losing money on interest is not an obvious, willful sin, but my "ends" policy of making God look good in my finances calls for some action since we are not keeping up with inflation in this economy. So I need to "work" on this matter. Here is my goal-planning worksheet.

Please remember that what seems most elementary to you is quite demanding to me, for various reasons. This is my life, demanding this kind of a mission for immediate attention, so that my ongoing effectiveness for God's glory can be sus-tained within a broad policy.

Notice also that these are not the *visionary* objectives yet to come in the next book of this series. This chart is useful in accomplishing those future visions as well. We are looking at *maintenance* issues in the routine running of life's segments, in integrating life's priorities. These are areas where you are responsible but are failing because of sin or neglect, areas in which God is not looking good in your life. You have identi-fied broad policies for these areas. They apply your values and communicate your perspectives, but you have not yet acted on them. Now you shall act, in order to accomplish the "mega-ends"[5] policy. The only end to which you aspire is glorifying God—the mission of life.

Yesterday my goal was to visit a friend suddenly admitted to the hospital. First, I had to make room for the visit in an overcrowded calendar. Second, I had to plan the time available for the visit. I allotted thirty minutes for the call. Ten minutes to go to the hospital and back, and ten minutes to encourage a very sick person and her family. Everything went by schedule. But uncontrollable factors included her getting worse in the middle of my prayer (that confirmed I don't possess the gift of healing!). They had to call for respiratory devices to attend her. I waited outside, but not frustrated, because I had built some time at the latter part of the visit for the unforeseen. Further, I have become increasingly convinced that God controls schedules, surprises, interruptions, and I seize personal peace in that conviction.

Oh! I just remembered that I need to get a physical examination soon. Physical life to the glory of God not only calls for appropriate eating and regular exercise, but also an annual medical examination. I've got to use the planning worksheet for what used to constitute a simple phone call. With all the new health insurance rules, calling your own doctor has become a major ordeal. Now I need to phone a primary care physician I don't know, to visit a doctor I have known for fifteen years! Increasing complexity will call for more planning.

INCREASING GOD'S WEIGHT

Look at your responsibilities, in all their dimensions, and place them under the glory of God. Increase God's weight in each area.

➤ Are you having a falling-out with your spouse? Love her or him. That brings God glory.

➤ Are you lazy in areas of life where you need to be a

better steward? Study God's Word for application in these areas and obey His commands. That bring God glory.

➤ Have you been giving primacy to secondary matters and peripheralizing important issues? Pray and ask for wisdom to prioritize better. That brings God glory.

I once counseled with a couple in South Africa, who were both crying for major attention from each other. As they looked at the schedule for the next three months, every night was taken by yet another good activity. Deep-seated anxieties surfaced and quick tempers flashed. As I listened to them, they were blatantly in violation of the weight of God in their lives, even though no one item in their packed calendars was an obvious violation. Neither of them was living in gross sin, but they had raised remote, tertiary demands to the status of a primary dimension. He left early each morning and came back very late each night. Business consumed him. She attempted to compensate spiritually for their relational breakdown and woke him up each morning at 5:30 to pray together. Needless to say, they hadn't processed life's segments under the glory of God and His weight in the three major dimensions.

Unable to see an end to their busyness, they were getting on each other's nerves. We looked at their schedule. Tuesday nights would open up after several weeks of taking a class. They would simply have to agree to bear with each other's temporary commitments until those eleven weeks were up, when they could plan on a vacation. Just talking about those two slight adjustments gave them a lift. Immediately their spirits revived. They acknowledged that they started enjoying each other again with firmer expectations of the future.

Missions in life deal with the regular responsibilities that we sustain in the breadth and depth of existence. These are the dailies, the weeklies, the yearlies—the routines which occupy our time. Our humanity limits us from omni-involvements. Good leaders though, while limited, are often very productive. Busy as they may be, they are able to prioritize, hierarchize, and realize the TARGET of their goals in action-biased, action-based intentional living. This kind of integrated living is part of redeeming the time during these evil days (Eph. 5:16), for there is no post-death opportunity to repeat life.

I would like to caution the dreamer, the castle-builder, anyone who merely lives in the future. It is alright to live off the future, like a bride waiting for wedding day, but don't live in the future. Too many Christians are waiting for the future and neglecting the present. They dream of future possibilities or live off prospects, while defaulting in their present responsibilities. When the present and future conflict, wholeheartedly attend to the present—your life, your spouse and kids, your relationships, your work. You've got to defend your missions in life—the three segments—so you can go on to capture a vision for life—the fourth segment. Your mission helps you defend the hill worth dying on.

Ecclesiastes reads,

Enjoy life with your wife, whom you love, all the days of this meaningless life that God has given you under the sun—all your meaningless days. For this is your lot in life and in your toilsome labor under the sun. Whatever your hand finds to do, do it with all your might, for in the grave, where you are going, there is neither working nor planning nor knowledge nor wisdom (Eccl. 9:9–10).

Colossians repeats that refrain:

Whatever you do, work at it with all your heart, as working for the Lord, not for men, since you know that you will receive an inheritance from the Lord as a reward. It is the Lord Christ you are serving (Col. 3:23–24).

The Intentional Life works itself out in the responsibilities of life under the lordship and glory of Christ. We ought not be fighting against air (1 Cor. 9:26), randomly and purposelessly. We ought to keep our spiritual fervor, serving the Lord (Rom. 12:11). I covet for us Moses' prayerful perspective on work found in Psalm 90:17, "May the favor of the Lord our God rest upon us; establish the work of our hands for us—yes, establish the work of our hands."

Furnishing Life

Realtors believe that selling homes depends, in part, on showing them . . . furnished. Empty rooms and bare walls seem less appealing to most buyers, even though they know they are not buying the furnishings, just the house. Spend a day participating in a "parade of open homes" and you'll find a generous assortment and an astounding variety in interior design. Whether curious or serious, you will be delighted by the creativity in decoration and presentation.

> The only true happiness comes from squandering ourselves for a purpose.
> ❧William Cowper

Each home welcomes you with an open door. Inside, tasteful furnishings beautify the rooms, make the environment pleasant and embellish the surroundings, without sacrificing function. Furniture pieces are not random accessories; they are necessities designed to help us enjoy and use the rooms within a home. Many other items from clocks to mirrors to wastebaskets present themselves to the creative designer-homemaker as expressions of beauty and utility. Even the decoration of the walls (whose structure and strength we placed under *passion*) flow over into decisions concerning furnishings, just as life-values flow into life-policies to be governed by life-virtues. For example, the role of truth in our lives can be as solid and functional as an unadorned wall, but when we speak the truth in love, we are highlighting passion with beauty.

Once upon a long time ago, our world actually assumed the necessity of character and integrity as requisites for personal, spiritual governance. In the current evil days, however, we live in a dark moral and ethical environment that places pragmatism above principle, expediency over truth, self over community. Gone is the expectation that virtue will permeate personality, temperament, and drivenness in our leaders. When U.S. President Clinton acknowledged inappropriate behavior to the world in mid-1998, his life began to ring hollow. Many people were not willing to take seriously his most important decisions in other areas. Others lauded his survival instincts as the "comeback" kid. In the President's case, the quality of risk-taking—a leader's basic trait—overflowed into immoral adventuresome-ness. People wanted to go forward and away from the scandal, but didn't want to forget it either. In these shameful circumstances, flawed character (dishonesty) undermined good missions (marriage and work).

Character functions like the built-in features and fixtures in a house that distinguish it from a mere, large box. Without it, life is empty of substance or full of stuff that might be kept there for storage or unintentional use, but possesses no vital connection with the structure. If you have raised your voice in an empty home, you probably heard echoes. There was nothing to absorb the sound. You need furniture, furnishings, and other fixtures to not hear the hollowness of an echo. If biblical values provide for the basic upkeep and prevent life's foundations from shifting, biblical *virtues* provide finishing touches and prevent a hollowness of life.[1]

VALUES NEED VIRTUES

By *virtues* we mean "that which makes life true, beautiful, and good." Virtues make life morally excellent. As one author puts it, "They are the substance of a happy life, that is, a life which embodies every quality required for a complete and flourishing human existence."[2] They are not simply ideals, but *practiced* ideals. Virtues provide the furnishings and fixtures of laudable character to the structure we call life. Daily mission, routine tasks, and ongoing relationships revolve around character. Preferred character furnishes the appropriate attitudes for accomplishing the tasks of life. Christian values without Christian virtues can easily result in sub-Christian living. Certain values of the Italian Mafia ("family loyalty" is also a Christian value), for example, can be admired. Without virtue, however, that value of family loyalty can become a twisted weapon of violence and injustice.

Let's face it. Virtues are not natural to us. Even if Christian values control us, it is possible to live out our values in the wrong way. This was unfortunately illustrated by a missionary who taught Christianity in Southern India. Reviewing what the students were supposed to know, he asked, "Why did Jesus come to the earth?" When they hesitated, he repeated the question, walking up and down the aisle hitting each child with a ruler on the head, yelling, "Love, love, love! That's why Jesus came into the world!" The teacher was certainly controlled by values. But virtue was tragically missing. His teaching methods spoke more loudly to his students than the content of his lessons.

Because virtues are infused from outside ourselves, they cannot be self-generated. We need conversion before transformation. Further, we receive the facility for biblical values and capacity for Christlike virtues at salvation. At that point, for the first time, there is the possibility that biblical values and Christlike virtues can be accomplished intentionally. Just as our pursuit of God as our ultra-value is intentional, the practice of Christian virtues takes spiritual deliberation. Before we knew Christ, we couldn't accomplish virtue even if we wanted to; with Christ, virtue becomes personally possible.

Virtues affect all of life. Just because I don't steal (negative virtue) doesn't mean that I serve like Jesus did (positive virtue). My associate gently sent me on a spiritual journey when he remarked, "You value biblical leadership patterns. Do you think your staff view you as a servant leader?" A tour of my actions yielded a sobering response to his question. My leadership value hadn't been governed by virtue. I was setting the example of honesty in detailed expense reports, but doing it without a servant's spirit. Yes, I wanted to do the right thing, but I needed to do the right thing in the right way. Values relate to the "right;" virtues relate to the "good—the right way." While you go about accomplishing your missions in life—personal, family, work—be sure that they are covered by Christlike virtues as well.

CORE VIRTUES

What Christlike virtues should accompany biblical values for accomplishing His prescriptions governing personal, family, and work life? I could go to several passages to find biblical virtues. Helpful checklists can be developed from the Beatitudes (Matt. 5), the Ten Commandments (Ex. 20), or the Love Chapter (1 Cor. 13).[3] Here, I point to Paul's statement about the fruit of the Spirit (Gal. 5:22–23) for a listing of spiritual virtues. I choose the fruit of the Spirit for the following reasons:

1) "Fruit" is a singular composite—it relates to all that we are, to a person's singular composition as well as to his or her varied responsibilities and interests.

2) "Fruit *of the Spirit*" acknowledges our utter inability to create, manipulate, merit, or achieve these virtues. We can only accomplish them by the power of the Spirit. It is God who declares us virtuous in salvation. It is also God who makes us virtuous in behavior. These are the works of the Holy Spirit in our lives as we continuously permit His control (Eph. 5:18).

Remember, the spiritual life is a God-thing, but it is also God's thing. We live by grace, allowing ourselves to be filled by the Spirit for the tasks of daily life. But we invite the power of the Holy Spirit to evidence itself in character as we are willing to obey him. Once more, the Trinity is the Governing Board, Jesus is the President, and I am the Executive Vice President of this brief life. I must be willing to submit to Him. Part of my submission to Him is putting habits into place, developing patterns for pleasing Him, and practicing godliness.

3) The nine fruit(s) listed reveal the kind of person we ought to be. They are a specific listing of the character of our Lord Jesus. He perfectly modeled love, joy, peace, patience, gentleness, goodness, faith, meekness, and self-control. The word "is" in the verse could be viewed as "attendant"— qualities or virtues attending those who walk by the Spirit and therefore do not fulfill the works of the flesh.

4) The fruit of the Spirit also gives us a way of measuring the evidence of our growth in the context of life missions.

Am I more loving today than I was yesterday? Last month? Last year? Am I more patient? What about self-control? While we do not want to find assurance of eternal salvation in these verses, we can certainly find evidence of spiritual growth in these nine traits.

Take some time to write out the meanings of each of these character words in spiritual and personal governance. I encourage you to consult a dictionary and a Bible dictionary. Looking up their meaning and reflecting on their significance will not only revitalize the mission in life-purpose, it will also give you character clues to attend the accomplishment of your mission. You could also look to see how the biblical author(s) used these words elsewhere. As you write out the definitions, ask the Holy Spirit to develop these character qualities in you. Put a spiritual strategy in place to live them out. (The list following is found in Galatians 5:22–23.)

Love:

_____

_____

Joy:

_____

_____

Peace:

_____

_____

Patience:

_____

_____

Kindness:

_____

_____

Goodness:

_____

_____

Faith(fulness):

_____

_____

Gentleness:

_____

_____

Self-control:

_____

_____

You have already encountered the "What?" "So What?" and "Now What?" study approach previously in this series. Let's use that format one more time as we analyze these words. For example, take meekness, used in the King James version, as more than a value, but as a virtue.

What?

Definitions for understanding meekness:

> English dictionary: "showing patience and humility" (American Heritage Collegiate Dictionary)
>
> *Synonyms:* "humble, docile, calm, tame, submissive" (Microsoft Word Thesaurus function)

Bible dictionary: "The high place accorded to meekness in the list of human virtues is due to the example and teaching of Jesus Christ. Pagan writers paid greater respect to the self-confident man. . . . In the New Testament meekness (*prautēs,* and adjective *praus*) refers to an inward attitude, whereas gentleness is expressed rather in outward action. It is part of the fruit of Christlike character produced only by the Spirit" ("Meekness," *New Bible Dictionary*).

My definition: "power under control." God wants me to exhibit the virtue of controlled power in my many mission relationships in family and work situations.

So What?

Questions for application:

1) In what areas do I find myself being less than meek?

   (I expect my wife to make her day's plans secondary to my demands on her.)

   (In my relationship with my older son, I care more for my ego than for him.)

2) Is there such a response as justifiable pride?

   Yes, when it doesn't relate to superiority over another person. I can find genuine joy in my older son's sacrificial giving to the Lord, my younger son's wrestling accomplishment, or my daughter's high school basketball records without negative pride.

3) How is meekness different from weakness?

   Weakness denotes spinelessness. Meekness is controlled power.

Now What?

Strategies for obedience:

1) To plan better so as not to impose sudden tasks on my wife. This would be progress in developing meekness. Begin by opening a file under my wife's name in my personal organizer, make entries, and consult it everyday before retiring for the night.

2) To genuinely care for colleagues and subordinates. I can ask questions about their personal needs before assigning functions or requesting help.

3) To incorporate the virtue of meekness under the Holy Spirit as a character trait, a lifestyle, and mindset, rather than simply applying that virtue to isolated acts.

Now you continue these exercises with all the fruit of the Spirit listed above, asking God for insight and influence for implementation.

THE POWER LINK

I was privileged to speak at the annual conference of the Union of Evangelical Baptists of Haiti in the northern part of that great land. Some of the Lord's grand saints live in this most impoverished country, barely a one-hour flight from the richest country in the world. No one who drives in Haiti misses the bathtub-size potholes. It seems like the roads in this country reflect the psyche of its people—torn, bumpy, gravelly, and unmapped. Traveling at about five miles per hour is not unusual. The final leg of our journey took eight-and-half hours to go about 100 miles. Along the way, we lost power in our vehicle's engine. Immediately, a friend jumped out of a truck in front of us and tied a heavy nylon strap to us. We had to be towed by this friend's truck for almost seven hours.

The only link between the two vehicles was a nylon webbing made to withstand about 40,000 pounds of tension. Where the tow truck chose to go, we followed. The truck driver was acutely aware that we were tied to and dependent on him. He had us in mind in every move he made—whether passing or stopping.

The driver of our vehicle did a superb job as he conscientiously followed the intentions of the tow truck driver and the movements of the tow truck. Our progress depended on two factors: remaining linked to the power source, and being willing to steer according to the lead truck. If either factor had failed, we might still be a Haiti roadside attraction.

I find the key components of virtuous vitality in accomplishing our life missions in this analogy. The two factors above mirror spiritual reality.

The first factor represents the importance of an ongoing, growing relationship with the One who possesses the power. A distinctive feature of our spiritual life is not only the command to do right, but also the *power* to do right in a perpetually and progressively developing relationship with God. In that spiritual connection lies the power. Our attachment to God is true but must be as real as that "unbreakable" webbing between the two vehicles in Haiti.

As we have already admitted, we simply do not possess the power to do right ourselves, let alone to do it in the right way. Yes, our mission directives are quite clear. I know that I must serve my employer as though I am serving the Lord; that I must raise my children in the nurture and discipline of the Lord; that I must carry out my vocation as God-pleaser and not as man-pleaser.

However, I also know I do not possess the power for these missions, nor the ability to fulfill them in the right way. I must be linked to the Power Source. This need calls on me to maintain a vital spiritual fellowship with God in all aspects (heart, soul, mind, and strength) *and* to practice biblical virtues in all of life's spheres. A God-valued life must go on, while the Christ-virtued life grows on. God's commands provide the outworking of our missions, and God's character shows the manner in which our mission is carried out. Together they make God look good in and through my life.

Earlier we used the metaphor of the Board, President, and Executive Vice President to describe the ongoing nature of our relations and responsibility under God. There is one large difference between the human parallel and spiritual reality. While the Trinitarian Board gives me wisdom for my way, and President Jesus confers authority for my responsibility, I am also given personal enablement and actual empowerment for their assignments. It is not only what I know, am, and do, but also who I have living in me and empowering me. And, yes, the Board and President also specialize in rescuing me from the aftermath of my stupidity. Then they resolve all of life in a final, eternal chapter.

Second, in the Haitian automobile analogy we focused on the "following" factor. We had enough say in the ride to go our own way, but not without dire consequences. We had enough control of our vehicle to strain the nylon chain. We could slow down when the truck wanted to move, or veer in a different direction than the lead vehicle. But we wanted to reach our destination and depended on the one leading us. The lead truck provided its power; all we brought to the progress was our cooperating desire.

And so it is with the God-life being God's thing. Through

faith we are tied to Him in an irrevocable, unbreakable bond. By His faithfulness, the salvation chain is secure. It cannot even be frayed. He provides the power by which we spiritually progress. We present our willingness to follow Him. We cannot accelerate the progress. But we can certainly decelerate the advance. We have enough say in the situation to follow, slow down, or veer. When we walk by the Spirit (Gal. 5:16), living by His resources, running on the track that He has set for us, not going outside the boundaries of this divine-human connection, we accomplish personal missions in spiritual ways. We will then exist for God's glory—the human mission—to make God look great.

Conclusion

I close this volume borrowing abbreviations from J. S. Bach, the early eighteenth-century organist and composer. As I write, his music fills my ears with the richest of sounds. Beady earphones supply the finer tones of his majestic concertos. He once commented on his remarkable musical accomplishments: "I have had to work hard; anyone who works just as hard will get just as far." You connect with that statement, I am sure.

You may also know that he signed off his compositions with *S.D.G.* Those who knew the abbreviation knew the connection of his mission in life—the vocation of music composition and directorship to the all-encompassing mission *of* life—*S.D.G.*—*Soli Deo Gloria.* His musical intentions were to make God look good. *Glory to God alone.*[1] That's the mission we want to pursue and implement in every area of life. At the end of every conversation, every talk, every chapter, every volume, I'd like to inscribe *S.D.G.*—my ulterior purpose. In every involvement, every pursuit, every relationship, every responsibility, I invite you to write *S.D.G.* in non-eraseable ink.

Bach's life was even more complex and busier than his prolific music. He fathered twenty children, ten of whom lived beyond childhood. He was also a teacher, administrator, and organ builder! Bach's multi-layered, multi-tasked, multi-gifted life (like yours) revealed another short form. He not only wrote S.D.G. but also J.J. on his music scores. Usually written at the beginning of his compositions, J.J. stood for *Jesu juva,* meaning "Help, O Jesus," or more precisely, "Help me, O Jesus."[2]

I open each workday by writing an expression of love to Jesus. Sometimes that expression is three sentences or even three pages long. On disheveled days when I am running fast, the expression turns into an exasperation with an exclamation mark, "Help, Lord Jesus!" And guess what? Jesus helps me make Him look better in my life's segments and surprises than I ever could do by myself in the middle of the muddle.

Consider this. If you pursue the practical exercises of this book, you will connect simplicity with complexity, values with tasks, policies with assignments, objectives with goals, knowledge with action, ends with aims. You will accomplish Bach's and your ulterior purpose—to make God look great—THE purpose. There is nothing better than "squandering" our lives for that great purpose.

In this trilogy thus far we have considered squandering our lives on two aspects of biblical purpose—"to love God" (*Soul Passion,* Book One) and "to honor God" (*Soul Mission,* Book Two). We now proceed to the final aspect of Christian purpose—"to serve God" (*Soul Vision,* Book Three). When a passion for Jesus Christ infuses your passions in life, and when a mission to glorify God fills your missions in life, you are well on your way to an intentional, well-built, profitable life. You will serve and excel in God's call to pursue a vision in your life that is compatible with His vision for the world. Book Three deals with your unique purpose in God's Vision: the *superstructure* of the Intentional Life. I look forward to your company as we continue this journey of reflection, exploration, and obedience.

Endnotes

Chapter 1: Anchoring Life

1. For readers outside the influence of British English, the first floor in India is called "ground" floor.

Chapter 2: Extending Passion, Framing Mission

1. Those following the construction analogy may have questions about basements and where they fit in the Intentional Life model. I offer these comments as a fascinating aside for those interested in developing the analogy further. Realize, however, that every illustration has limits.

   I once stayed in an Indianapolis home with a basement —that wonderful, special part of a home not normally available in clay-dominated North Texas. When their family found extra time during the week, weekend, or vacation, they hastened down a carpeted staircase to relish life and each other. Here they played pool, table tennis, board games, watched TV, exercised, stepped out the back door to swim, and came back to the basement counter for refreshments. Seldom did they do the tedious, the onerous, or the ponderous down there. Breaks in schedule and responsibilities called for more time in the basement. They bemoaned not being able to spend more time in this less-cluttered and fun-filled area in their house. That midwestern basement revealed several true interests of my host family—what they enjoyed, loved, and pursued as life's goals.

   The blessing of basement space is that you can use it for the extra "whatever." Basements show what you would rather do. They reveal the larger desires for which you live, disclose where you spend discretionary time and money, and recharge you for the upcoming week. They communicate some of your real interests and store some of your treasures. In the case of my hosts what they did upstairs and outside were simply means to allow what they did in the room below, inside. Spending time downstairs was fulfilling a desire. What they did down in the basement helped them to function better above and outside, which in turn made the basement time possible.

   Cellars also double up as storm shelters. Basements preserve people through storms. My hosts recalled people taking refuge in basements when tornadoes devastated Indiana in the mid-1900s. Another beautiful analogy emerged. You must be ready to retreat to your spiritual basement at the first storm warning. Uncontrollable weather patterns strike without gaining permission. Stay down there for relief. Read and pray over the Scriptures to gain energy till the storm passes by. Scriptures provide the mandate and the motivation for passion.

   The basement, then, can reveal the locus of your passion(s), your goals, and the various ways the structure above is connected to the bedrock below. It is a repository, a refuge, and a resource for life. You can't live there all the time, but if you don't enjoy its resources, your life is affected. If you enjoy frequent visits, they increase the quality of your life. Its promise of joy strengthens you during the day. But its provision of strength helps you through the week. The hidden room beneath energizes, heightens, and intensifies life above.

   The basement performs the functions and provides the benefits of passion(s). You find space for energy storage, safe zones, and renewed strength for upcoming and unpredictable challenges. Yet not all houses feature basements. In Texas we hide under beds and inside bathtubs when tornadoes break. We may find shelter in these alternate havens, but we have to find extra space for basement equivalents. But all houses, even in Texas, must feature floors, walls, and ceilings—again analogies for functions of passion in the Christian life.

2. Other parts of personal identity can be constituted from a view of our salvation (forgiveness of sins); our spirituality (love and service for God); our origins (where have we came from?); our meaning and purpose (why are we here?); and destiny (where are we going?) All of these aspects of our identity flow out of our relationship with God through the Lord Jesus Christ.

3. Later we will distinguish between the mission "of" life and missions "in" life, as well as the vision "of" life and visions "in" life.

4. "Where to Herr Messner?" *Lufthansa Magazin,* October 1998, pp.30-3?

Chapter 3: Sole Mission

1. Judges allow changing a name if they are convinced that a person doesn't intend to cover felonious tracks or deceive the Internal Revenue Service!

2. Summarized from "Bigger Than a Breadbox, or Anything Else," *New York Times,* 9 January 2001 A16. "We have found nothing bigger in literature and nobody has brought to our attention anything bigger," said Gerard Williger, a National Optical Astronomy Observatories researcher at a meeting of the American Astronomical Society. And the very next day the headlines read, "Found: 2 Planetary Systems. Result: Astronomers Stunned," questioning "the very meaning of the term 'planet.' . . . We never expected nature would make such gargantuan planets, and maybe they are not planets at all." (*New York Times,* 10 January 2001, A1, 16). Of course, nature did not make them, they were God's play time, God's fingerwork! Our understanding of the sheer numbers and structures keep changing, deepening, widening so much all the time that I hate to put those details into print!

3. You may know that the tetragrammaton, *YHWH* (usually pronounced Yahweh), is a contraction of YaHoWaH, where the vowels are borrowed from another Old Testament name for God—*adon-ai.* In this way, each time the faithful saw *YHWH,* they would use *adonai* in keeping with Jewish inclination to hold God's name sacred in mind and speech.

Chapter 4: Soul Mission

1. First attributed to Donald Weinstein, Fair Lawn, N.J., quoted in Lawrence Van Gelder, "The Office as Comedy Club," *New York Times,* 7 July 1996, 8F.

2. My mail recently advertised a new book titled *The Richards Since the Civil War,* created just for me, tracing the Richards' unique genealogy to those who were born and died in America over the past century. The pitch was based on the premise that names are important to identity. The gimmick letter was signed by my long lost, long-distance cousin, Francine P. Richard, unaware that I have only been in and out of America for two decades and my father is the first Richard in our family line!

3. Advertising campaign run by *Partnership for a Drug-Free America,* seen 2001–2002.

4. Note how unskeptically we assume the role of questioner illustrated, for example, by Carl Sagan and Ann Druyan, "What Makes Us Different?" *Parade Magazine,* 20 September 1992.

5. Read the powerful conclusion of *Wrinkles in Time* by George Smoot and Keay Davidson (New York: William Morrow and Co., 1993), the chapter titled "Toward the Ultimate Question" (pp. 272–97) to come very, very close to a scientific acknowledgment of the God "metaphor." I prefer God's "fingerwork" as the metaphor, with God as the only, ultimate, cosmological explanation of the universe—the scientist shall yield at the final threshold to the theologian.

6. Some biblical scholars also see the animal-human distinction in the *means* of human creation, for it took God's hand (Gen. 2:7), unlike everything else which was brought into existence by God's word, and in a special endowment of God's breath (Gen 2:7; but see Gen. 1:30), giving humans spiritual capacity for understanding the Almighty (cf. Job 32:8).

Chapter 5: Theologizing Life

1. I can't press the observation too hard, but "smoke" seems to portray the visible holiness of God, as in Isaiah 6, while "cloud" manifests the visible presence of God (cf. Ex. 40:33–35; 1 Kings 8:10–12). The phenomena assaulted the senses of the worshiper.

2. "The rock foundation on which Christ would build his church was the eternal, unchangeable truth of the confession of Christ." (From W. Mundle, "Rock," under petra, "petra," in *Dictionary of New Testament Theology,* Vol. 3:385, Colin Brown, ed. [Grand Rapids, Mich.: Zondervan, 1986]).

3. The implications of God's Holy-Love maintain the soil around the salvation foundation. The spiritual disciplines of detachment and alignment (which we will discuss a little later) revolve around God's expectation of holiness. Those of attachment and engagement are empowered and motivated by love in response to God's love for us.

4. For instance, "In Niger, as in many other places in Africa, fat is the beauty ideal for women." From "On the Scale of Beauty, Weight Weighs Heavily," *New York Times,* 12 February 2001, A4.

5. R. L. Harris, *Theological Wordbook of the Old Testament* (Chicago: Moody, 1980), pp. 426, 943g.

6. Story found in Douglas V. Steere, *Doors into Life* (New York: Harper, 1948), pp. 138–39.

Chapter 6: Vectoring Life

1. Paul Goldberger, "Saluting a Building by a Man Who Stirs Things Up," *New York Times,* 14 October 1996. The critic rightly asks: "Was the Center intended to grab attention more than to solve a problem? Did it mark the final gasp of modernism, or the beginning of something else? Did it symbolize the breaking of barriers between inside and outside, or the blurring of form and function; was it the modest building its architect somewhat disingenuously pretended it was, or the ultimate expression of a powerful ego?"

2. I find the confusion even in good books. For example, *LifeKeys* by Jane A. G. Kise, David Stark, Sandra Krebs Hirsh (Minneapolis: Bethany, 1996) argues: "Jesus knew his mission. . . . Have you identified your mission?" (p. 209).

3. Paul echoes the conscience of completion as well, when he stated, "I consider my life worth nothing to me, if only I may finish the race and complete the task the Lord Jesus has given me—the task of testifying to the gospel of God's grace" (Acts 20:24). "I have finished the race" (2 Tim. 4:7). He went about preaching the kingdom of God (Acts 20:25), a mission not too different from Jesus' own mandate. Paul and Timothy carried on the work of the Lord: "If Timothy comes, see to it that he has nothing to fear while he is with you, for he is carrying on the work of the Lord, just as I am" (1 Cor. 16:10).

4. Many spirituality theories make the lifelong pursuit of the purpose of life as the purpose of life! Some philosophies claim with F. Scott Fitzgerald that, "the meaning of life is that there is no meaning." Yet other religions make union with God the purpose of life. By strained mental, physical, or ritual effort, one hopes to attain the religious purpose(s) of life. Further, mysticism assumes a continuum between humanity and God, but spiritual relationship with God must be established before it can be spiritual. In the Bible, one doesn't have to spend a lifetime establishing a connection with God. Through Jesus, an eternal relationship with God is established. One's mission becomes glorifying God who has already initiated spiritual connection with humanity and establishes it with believers.

5. This resolution strategy is practiced by Moses' mother (Ex. 2:3–9), Mordecai (Est. 3:2), Esther (Est. 4:13–16), and the three Hebrew children (Dan. 3:16–18).

6. The attempts of theoretical physicists to capture the nature of the underlying reality in a complete unified theory have traversed from superstrings to supermembranes to open membrane (OM) theories. The Bible lodges it in a super-Person, in whom "all things hold together" (Col. 1:17), or as the King James Version puts it, "by him all things consist," so that "in all things he might have the preeminence" (Col. 1:17, 18).

7. Condensed from Larry Rohter, "For the Mailmen Lost in a Maze, Amazing News," *New York Times,* 15 November 1996, A6.

8. We will add a fourth segment later, placing "ministry life" into a category of its own by our need to align with God's *vision* for the world.

Chapter 7: Integrating Life

1. Jacques Steinberg, "At College Graduations, Wit and Wisdom for the Price of Airfare," *New York Times*, 28 May 2001, A10.

2. "Policies" are *the values or perspectives that underlie action.* (From John Carver and Miriam Mayhew Carver, *Reinventing Your Board: A Step-by-Step Guide to Implementing Policy Governance* [San Francisco: Jossey Bass, 1997], p. 17). While John Carver is a foremost authority on corporate boards (also see his *Boards That Make a Difference: A New Design for Leadership in Nonprofit and Public Organizations* (San Francisco: Jossey-Bass, 1997), and certainly there are differences, I see wise connections between Carver's corporate governance and personal governance.

3. The "want list" is recommended by Kevin McCarthy, *The On-Purpose Person: Making Your Life Make Sense* (Colorado Springs: Piñon Press, 1992).

4. Ibid., pp. 44–51.

5. McCarthy says, "Go with your instincts, yet be patient and thoughtful. Think it through" (*The On-Purpose Person,* p. 50).

6. Several versions of this parable are floating on the Internet, some as early as Charles Spurgeon (1834–1892) including one from Stephen R. Covey's book, *First Things First* (New York: Fireside/Simon & Schuster, 1996), pp. 88–89.

Chapter 8: T.A.R.G.E.T.-ing Life

1. Michael Robert, *Strategy Pure and Simple: How Winning CEO's Outthink their Competition* (New York: McGraw-Hill, 1993), p. 85. He continues, "On the other side of the battlefield, the hill on the right and in the middle are not important, but the one on the left must be captured because it will give an unobstructed view of the other half of the battlefield. The same concept applies to business."

2. Peter F. Drucker, *Management: Tasks, Responsibilities, Practices* (New York: Harper & Row, 1973), p. 119.

3. I suggest that in areas of sin—by neglect, misuse, or lack of discipline—that you write out objectives for ongoing, long-term obedience to God. These can be done as a result of your passion in the passion section pursuit of the spiritual disciplines that we introduced in Book One, or here in making God look great through your life.

4. Found while I pastored a church in New Delhi, India and adopted for personal, family, and organizational use. Slightly revised from my first acquaintance with it in Norman Shawchuck and Lloyd M. Perry, *Revitalizing the Local Church* (Chicago: Moody, 1982).

5. John Carver, *Boards that Make a Difference: A New Design for Leadership in Nonprofit and Public Organizations,* 2nd ed. (San Francisco: Jossey Bass, 1997), p. 58.

Chapter 9: Furnishing Life

1. We introduce *virtue* to *value* at this point, because we don't want to reduce value to mere "emotion"—what we care most about. "Passion" is more than psychological. When passion is unleashed into mission, we must include moral dimensions with emotional fervor, spiritual output to personal feeling.

2. Romanus Cessario, O.P., *The Moral Virtues and Theological Ethics* (Notre Dame: University of Notre Dame Press, 1991), p. 4. See also his *Christian Faith & the Theological Life* (Washington, D.C.: The Catholic University of America Press, 1996) for the application of virtues to the Christian life. Theological virtues are faith, hope, and charity. Moral virtues are prudence, justice, fortitude, and temperance. All these can only be operable by grace, through faith, and in the power of the Holy Spirit. Some thinkers add intellectual virtues, which are also available to non-Christians.

3. In Jonathan R. Wilson, *Gospel Virtues: Practicing Faith, Hope & Love in Uncertain Times* (Downers Grove, IL: InterVarsity, 1998) he theologically builds on St. Paul's final trio in 1 Corinthians 13.

Conclusion

1. From Bernard S. Greenberg at www.bachfaq.org/sdg (1999, 2000). Greenberg states: *"Soli Deo Gloria* means 'To God alone (be) (the) Glory.' Note that Latin does not employ articles (a, the), so it is ambiguous as to whether it refers to all glory in general, or the glory that is reflected in the piece currently being so dedicated. The verb (to be) is implied. Bach would often write this at the end of a composition. Stephen Daw, writing in the *Oxford Composer Companion: Bach,* expands the initials as *Sit Deo Gloria,* 'To God be (the) Glory.'" Elsewhere Bach wrote, "The aim and final end of all music should be none other than the glory of God and refreshment of the soul. If heed is not paid to this, it is not true music but a diabolical bawling and twanging."

2. Ibid. *"Juva* is the singular imperative form of *juvare,* 'to help,' so it is a request for help ('help me'). *Jesu* is the 'vocative form' of *Jesus,* meaning 'O Jesus', so 'Help me, O Jesus' might be the best translation. Bach would write this near the beginnings of works." In Latin, J. was also a symbol for prayer."

About the Author

Dr. Ramesh Richard is a professor at Dallas Theological Seminary, where he teaches expository preaching, the spiritual life, and worldview apologetics. He is also the founder and president of *RREACH* International, through which God has permitted him to serve as a global spokesman for the Lord Jesus Christ.

RREACH is an acronym for Ramesh Richard Evangelism and Church Helps. A global proclamation ministry, the vision of *RREACH* is to change the way *one billion individuals* think and hear about the Lord Jesus Christ. Its mission is to "proclaim the Lord Jesus Christ worldwide, with a strategic burden for strengthening the pastoral leaders and evangelizing the opinion leaders of weaker economies."

From his platform at *RREACH*, Dr. Richard travels throughout the world, clarifying the message of the Bible. His audiences are wide-ranging—from non-Christian intellectuals at Harvard University to poor pastors in Haiti, from gatherings of a few to a hundred thousand. In recent years he has been speaking to crowds of men about their spiritual responsibilities in stadiums across the United States. The Lord has given him the opportunity to train thousands of church leaders in more than seventy countries to preach, live and think biblically. He also has the privilege of exposing society's "opinion leaders" to the Lord Jesus Christ. Each New Year's Day he presents the gospel on prime-time, secular television to large numbers of English-speaking, internet active audiences in about one hundred countries.

A theologian, philosopher-expositor, evangelist, and author, Dr. Richard holds a Th.D. in Systematic Theology from Dallas Theological Seminary, and a Ph.D. in Philosophy from the University of Delhi.

He lives in the Dallas, Texas, area with his wife, Bonnie their children, Ryan, Robby, and Sitara.

Order Dr. Ramesh Richard's

"Life Rocks"

DVD/Video summary of

THE INTENTIONAL LIFE

from RREACH International
www.rreach.org

5500 West Plano Parkway, Suite 100, Plano, TX 75093
Telephone: 972-733-3402; Fax 972-733-3495;
Email: info@rreach.org

The Intentional Life Trilogy

ISBN: 0-8024-6460-2

Soul Passion is a response to the need Dr. Ramesh Richard sees for believers to pursue a purpose so lofty and yet so solid that the shifting sands of daily life will never be able to keep us from living each day in light of our soul passion, our ultimate purpose.

Through his wide-angle lens of international travel, his eye firmly on the compass of biblical truth, Dr. Richard leads his readers on a not-to-be-missed literary hike through familiar terrain, making it seem like the first time ever. Get on board!

> Howard G. Hendricks, Distinguished Professor, Chairman,
> Center for Christian Leadership, Dallas Theological Seminary

MOODY
PUBLISHERS

THE NAME YOU CAN TRUST.

1-800-678-6928 www.MoodyPublishers.org

Since 1894, Moody Publishers has been dedicated to equip and motivate people to advance the cause of Christ by publishing evangelical Christian literature and other media for all ages, around the world. Because we are a ministry of the Moody Bible Institute of Chicago, a portion of the proceeds from the sale of this book go to train the next generation of Christian leaders.

If we may serve you in any way in your spiritual journey toward understanding Christ and the Christian life, please contact us at www.moodypublishers.com.

*"All Scripture is God-breathed and is useful
for teaching, rebuking, correcting and training in
righteousness, so that the man of God may be
thoroughly equipped for every good work."*
—2 TIMOTHY 3:16, 17

MOODY
PUBLISHERS

THE NAME YOU CAN TRUST®

SOUL MISSION TEAM

ACQUIRING EDITOR:
Greg Thornton

COPY EDITOR & INTERIOR DESIGN:
Livingstone Corporation

BACK COVER COPY:
Julie-Allyson Ieron, Joy Media

COVER DESIGN:
UDG| DesignWorks

PRINTING AND BINDING:
Quebecor World Book Services

The typeface for the text of this book is
Sabon